The Baseball Life of
Mickey Mantle

by John Devaney

illustrated with photographs

Cover photograph by Wide World

SCHOLASTIC BOOK SERVICES
NEW YORK • TORONTO • LONDON • AUCKLAND • SYDNEY

FOR BARBARA, MOTHER OF TWO

Copyright © 1969 by John Devaney. All rights reserved. Published by Scholastic Book Services, a division of Scholastic Magazines, Inc.

1st printing . . . . March 1969

Printed in the U. S. A.

CONTENTS

1

Mick: The Champion Who Should Never Have Been

H E WALKED SLOWLY toward the plate, an embarrassed grin on his face. At the first sight of that broad-shouldered player, fans began yelling and cheering. The announcer's voice boomed: "Coming to bat for the New York Yankees . . . Number 7 . . . Mickey Mantle!" and the fans shouted, roared, and stamped their feet, then waited tensely for the pitch.

Mantle, facing a lefthander from the right-hand batter's box, ducked his head and dug his spikes into the dirt. He flicked his bat once, twice. The pitcher took the sign, swooped into his windup, and threw a hopping, humming fast ball.

Mantle's bat lashed out — *c-r-a-c-k*. The crowd stood up to watch the ball soar toward the center-field wall. The center fielder started toward it, then stared helplessly as the ball zoomed thirty feet over his head into the bleacher seats.

Home run! Yankee Stadium exploded in sound. Over 40,000 people screamed, as with an easy-going, yet surprisingly fast gait, Mantle rounded second, then third, and trotted home.

As the crowd roared its approval, his Yankee teammates rushed out to congratulate him. They slapped Mickey on the back and hugged him, shook his hand. Mick, as the Yankees called Mantle, had hit another. Mick had won another ball game. Mick had come through again.

Mickey Charles Mantle has hit more home runs than anyone playing in the American League today. Only two men in baseball history have hit more home runs in their careers.

Mickey Mantle has also played in more games as a Yankee than any player in history — more than Joe DiMaggio, Babe Ruth, Yogi Berra, anyone. In fact, he has played in more World Series games than any outfielder in history. Three times he has been named the American League's Most Valuable Player. And one day Mickey Mantle will join the greatest stars of all time — in baseball's Hall of Fame.

Mickey is liked and admired by his Yankee teammates. Here they congratulate him as he crosses home plate on a homer.

But Mickey is more than a great ballplayer. He is a great team man too. "As Mickey Mantle goes, so go the Yankees." For years fans have said it and they just may be right.

"When Mickey comes into the line-up," Bobby Richardson, former Yankee second baseman, once said, "we are a different ball club. When he is in there we feel nobody is going to beat us."

"When Mickey's playing well," said Elston Howard, a Yankee catcher during Mickey's greatest years, "his actions kind of spill over on everybody. Just to know he is in the line-up, ready to swing with somebody on base, gives a ball club like ours a lift it needs. He is the kind of player who is so good himself, it makes everybody want to follow his example."

Mickey's rage to win has actually pulled the Yankees out of defeat and driven them to victory. In 1960 the Pirates beat the Yankees in the World Series. After the game Mickey sat in front of his locker, actually *crying*. The sight shocked the other Yankees. And the following season the Yankees wrecked the National League representative, the Cincinnati Reds, in five games. "We won it so easily," third baseman Clete Boyer said later, "because everyone on the team knew how badly Mickey wanted to beat the National League and make up for 1960."

During all his days as a Yankee, Mickey has wanted one thing — to be treated as one of the gang. No different, no better, though he was a star almost from the first. And he doesn't like to be singled out for special attention. If photographers want his picture after a game, Mickey often asks that another player, who has also helped to win, join him for the picture.

Yet, as much as he has always wanted to be one of the gang, Mickey could never be just another ballplayer — not to the Yankees, who admire him so much, and not to the fans, either. Mickey's skills and greatness on the field are part of the reason. And so is the kind of person he is.

Tom Tresh and Joe Pepitone watched Mantle for years from bleacher seats and in front of television sets. "When you get real close to someone after idolizing them from afar," Tresh once told me, "you would think your opinion of them would come down a little bit. I mean, when you see someone every day — day in and day out — it would figure you would see them do things that would make you think less of them. But now

9

that I'm close to Mantle, my opinion of him hasn't gone down at all. In fact, it's gone up."

Mantle is the sort of man who can be great on the ball field, and yet takes time to be kind and considerate off the field. But there is still another side of Mantle's greatness. It is a special kind of heroism — the will to carry on in spite of physical handicaps. It is what one ballplayer meant when he said: "Mickey Mantle is a champion who should never have been."

Still, Mantle was born into baseball. . . .

2

Mutt's Ambition: A Big-League Switch-Hitter

GRIPPING THE BAT, five-year-old Mickey waited for the pitch. When it came, he swung left-handed, awkwardly. He missed. He swung again. And missed. He swung a third time. And missed. For fifteen minutes he swung left-handed. He hit nothing.

Mickey wanted to quit. His dad said No, Mickey was to stay at the plate and continue swinging left-handed.

For two weeks, from four o'clock in the evening until late each evening, Mickey swung — right-handed against the left-handed pitches of his grandfather, then left-handed against the right-handed pitches of his father. Mickey loved to swing righty. He hated to swing lefty.

Then, one day, Mickey caught hold of a pitch, batting lefty, and drove it straight down what would have been the right-field line in a game. Mickey's face glowed. Maybe this idea of batting left-handed wasn't so bad after all.

Mutt Mantle smiled when he saw Mickey rip that line drive. At that time — the year was 1936 — a switch-hitter was as scarce in baseball as oysters in a desert. Mutt had the idea his boy would have a much better chance of becoming a big leaguer if he could switch-hit — and a big leaguer was what Mutt and Mickey's grandfather were determined Mickey would be.

Mutt's real name was Elven, but most everyone called him Mutt, a nickname for a natural ballplayer. A big, rawboned six-footer, Mutt Mantle had wanted to be a big-league hitter himself. But early in life he had gone to work to support his family. He had spent most of his life as a miner, clawing at rock in lead and zinc mines hundreds of feet underground. Only on Sundays did he play baseball, on small-town dusty fields a long way from the big-league diamonds where he had dreamed of playing.

So, long before his first child was born, Mutt Mantle promised himself he would train his son to be a big leaguer. No miner's life for his child — and no minor leagues either.

Mickey Charles Mantle was born on October 20, 1931, just a few weeks after the 1931 World Series. Mutt Mantle had read story after story about that Series in the Oklahoma newspapers. He was rooting for the Philadelphia Athletics against the St. Louis Cardinals, and even after the Cardinals beat the Athletics, Mutt Mantle continued to root for his hero, Philadelphia's catcher Mickey Cochrane.

So, of course his first child — a boy — was named Mickey. Mutt Mantle wanted his son to be as great a player as his namesake, Mickey Cochrane. Almost every day Mutt would flip a rubber ball into Mickey's cradle. Once, when Mickey was about a year old, he accidentally nabbed a ball thrown by his dad. Mutt laughed happily. "I'll bet," he said, "that Mickey Cochrane wasn't half as good at his age."

Now, at five, Mickey was learning to swat baseballs left-handed and right-handed — something Mickey Cochrane could never do. Batting right-handed against his grandfather's left-handed tosses, Mickey smacked long drives over the roof of the Mantle house. But batting left-handed, he often swatted empty air.

Mickey didn't really like batting lefty. It

13

was much more fun to smack those long drives than to strike out swinging left-handed. But he learned, and he grew better all the time.

No one in Commerce, Oklahoma, where they lived, could run bases faster. "It's no surprise," people said. "Mickey's mother ran so fast in school she could beat most of the boys. And who do you know who can run faster than Mutt Mantle?"

Mickey could bat and he could run. But his first position on a baseball team was catcher, like his namesake Mickey Cochrane. When he was ten he caught for a team in a peewee division of a junior baseball league. Even for his age Mickey was a peewee — one of the smallest boys in his class. His mother recalled how Mickey used to look as a peewee catcher. "When he squatted down behind the plate," she said, "wearing that protector that was too big for him, you couldn't see his feet, and about all you could see of him, except for his arms, were those two little eyes sticking out of the protector, like a scared turtle looking out of its shell."

The "turtle," though, soon led the peewee division in hitting. Each night, after a game, Mickey ran to meet his dad coming home from his job at the Blue Goose Mine.

Excitedly, Mickey told Mutt about the triple he had hit, the base he had stolen, or the runner he had thrown out trying to steal.

In his autobiography, *The Education of a Baseball Player,* Mickey wrote of his father: "No boy, I think, ever loved his father more than I did. . . . I would do nearly anything to keep my father happy. . . . He never had to raise his hand to me to make me obey, for I needed only a sharp look and a word from him and the knowledge that I had displeased him to make me go and do better.

". . . I knew from the time I was small that every small victory I won, and every solid hit I made or prize I was awarded, brought real joy to my father's heart. . . ."

Mutt Mantle was most displeased when Mickey grumbled about swinging left-handed. And even after seven years of trying to bat both lefty and righty, Mickey still was a .400 hitter right-handed; a .200 hitter left-handed.

In one game in the peewee league, Mickey batted left-handed against the right-handed pitcher and struck out three times in a row. On his fourth at bat, Mickey came to the plate and stepped into the right-hand hitter's box.

The pitcher wound up and threw. Mickey

swung and missed. "Strike one," yelled the umpire.

Then Mickey heard another yell. It was his father. "Go on home," he shouted, "and don't you ever put on that uniform again until you switch-hit like I told you."

Mickey dropped the bat and ran home.

Never again did Mickey try to bat righty against a righty pitcher. He was going to be a switch-hitter just as his father wanted him to be. Mickey later told boys who came to him for advice: "Anybody can develop into a switch-hitter if you start early enough — at ten, twelve, even in your early teens."

When Mickey was fourteen, he began to shoot up in height. He grew stronger too. And he could run faster than ever. "There was not a boy or man in town who could outrun me," he said later.

Mutt Mantle soon realized that Mickey was too fast to be a catcher — even a catcher like Mickey Cochrane. So Mickey Mantle switched to pitching, zipping fast balls past startled pitchers. In high school he was a star pitcher, sometimes striking out sixteen or seventeen batters in a game.

His high school coach, though, figured Mickey played best at second base. Later he switched Mickey to shortstop, and Mickey would gun throws to first base to nip runners trying to beat out base hits.

A natural shortstop? Not quite. When a ground ball bounced straight at Mickey, his arms would suddenly go stiff, and often the ball would bounce off his rigid glove. At other times, when Mickey caught the ball, he would throw it twenty feet over the first baseman's head. "And we had some pretty tall first basemen," Mickey jokes, remembering those days.

Mickey often felt he was a worse ballplayer than any of his friends. Still, he refused to give up. After the game he'd go home and spend hours practicing with his dad. Mutt Mantle would tap hundreds of ground balls at his son, and Mickey would throw them back — slowly, ever so slowly, learning how to scoop up the ball and throw accurately to first.

When the high school season ended in the spring of 1946, Mickey joined the Miami (Oklahoma) team in the Ban Johnson League, an amateur league for teenagers. One day Mickey's team met the nearby Baxter Springs Whiz Kids. Mickey came to the plate with the bases filled and nobody out.

The pitcher's first pitch was a fast ball. Mickey didn't let it go by. He hit it on a

At fourteen, Mickey played for the Miami, Oklahoma, amateur team. Until his senior year, Mickey was small for his age.

low line over the second baseman's head. The right fielder dashed in and caught the ball at his shoe tops. He whistled the ball to second base, doubling up one runner, and then the shortstop snapped a throw to first. Mickey had slammed into his first triple play.

After the game the manager of the Whiz Kids, Barney Barnett, strolled over to Mutt Mantle. Barney had been impressed by the ferocity of Mickey's line drive. "I'd like Mickey to play for the Whiz Kids next year, Mutt," Barney said to his old friend.

"If it's O.K. with Mickey, it's O.K. with me," said Mutt.

But baseball wasn't Mickey's only sport. He starred in basketball and football too. In basketball games for Commerce High, he popped in long set shots. Ralph Terry, a former Yankee pitcher who went to a high school not far from Commerce, still remembers Mickey's outstanding performance in high school basketball.

As for Mickey's football skills, Commerce fans thought Mickey a Gale Sayers kind of running back. "In my opinion," said John Lingo, Mickey's high school football coach, "baseball was Mickey's second-best sport. He was the best high school football player I ever saw."

Mickey ran through the opponent's lines with a high-stepping, ferocious stride. He weighed only 140 to 160 pounds during his four years in high school, but he smashed into tacklers with the brute force of a runaway truck. He ran, he passed, he kicked for Commerce.

One of Mickey's best friends was Bill Bosely, a hard-driving halfback. From Bill, Mickey learned how to crash into lines with his knees pumping like jackhammers, his feet bouncing off the ground. "He runs," another player once said of Mickey, "like a man whose feet hurt."

Mickey made tacklers hurt as he churned through their arms for long fifty-yard gains. His father came to the games to watch Mickey. But he wasn't happy about Mickey's playing football. "You can hurt your legs playing this game," Mutt Mantle told his son. "Then you won't be able to play baseball."

But Mickey wanted to play football — a game he still watches. One day the Commerce Tigers were scrimmaging. Mickey took the ball and rammed into the line. Someone slammed into him and he went down. A stray foot kicked Mickey's left shin.

Mickey got to his feet, rubbing his shin, a

painful grimace on his face. He limped back to the huddle. Later, in the shower, he massaged the shin. It still hurt a lot. He came home with a gimpy leg. His mother had him soak the leg in hot water, and the pain seemed to ebb away.

But that night it flared anew. From midnight on, Mickey tossed in bed with the shin throbbing. In the morning he noticed that his ankle had swollen. It looked like a dirty-blue softball. Mickey called his father, who took one look at the ankle and gulped.

Quickly he bundled Mickey into a car and sped to the doctor's. The doctor examined the ankle and suggested they drive to nearby Picher, Oklahoma, to have X rays taken. At Picher a bone specialist studied the X rays of Mickey's ankle and then talked in a corner with Mutt Mantle.

"Your son," said the doctor, "has osteomyelitis."

"What does that mean?"

"Osteomyelitis is a bone infection," said the doctor. "We can treat it and help it but we can't cure it."

"You mean he'll always have it?"

"With treatment the pain and swelling will disappear. But it could come back. It could come back if your son bruises the leg even slightly."

"My son is a ballplayer. A good ballplayer. What do you suggest I do?"

The specialist proposed taking Mickey to Oklahoma City where some of the best doctors in the midwest could give him treatment. A glum Mickey and Mutt drove to Oklahoma City. "When it finally dawned on me," Mickey said later, "that possibly I would be forced to forget about baseball, football, and any other sports, I thought I'd go crazy."

In an Oklahoma City hospital, doctors studied the swollen ankle. They injected drugs into it. But the ankle still throbbed with pain. It still looked dark and ugly.

Mickey and Mutt watched the doctors who talked with each other in low tones. Were these men going to say that Mickey could never play ball again?

3

A Chance to Be a Yankee

MICKEY WAS BACK HOME with his family — his younger twin brothers, Roy and Ray; his little sister Barbara; the baby Larry; and his mother and father. Gloomily, Mickey slumped in a chair in the living room. Next to him rested a pair of crutches. After two weeks of treatment in Oklahoma City, the swelling had gone down. But the doctors had warned him: any slight injury could puff up the ankle. "Take it easy," they had said.

Take it easy? They were talking about *Mickey Mantle,* who loved baseball and football and basketball — and all sports. How *could* he take it easy?

His father stared out the window. He was terribly disappointed too. But Mickey needed cheering up. What could Mutt do to give his son a boost? Suddenly Mutt had an idea.

"Mick," he said, turning around, "how would you like to get in the car and drive to St. Louis?"

At Sportsman's Park in St. Louis, Missouri, the Cardinals and Red Sox were soon to tangle in the 1946 World Series.

Mickey grabbed the crutches and lifted himself up. Sure he would like to go. When could they start?

A few days later Mickey sat in the grandstand with his father, some 300 miles from home, watching his first World Series game. He saw the Red Sox win, 3-2, when big Rudy York slammed out a home run in the tenth inning. The next day he cheered as the Cardinals won 3-0.

A very different Mickey rode back to Commerce. He felt happier and more alive than he had in a long time. And he could hardly stop grinning, for next to the Yankees, the Cardinals were his favorite team.

Back home, Mickey listened to the radio with growing excitement, as the Cardinals and Red Sox fought down to the seventh game of the Series. In that game the Cardinals' Enos Slaughter ran all the way home from first base on a single to score the winning run. The Cardinals had won the 1946 World Series.

In the excitement of that World Series Mickey had forgotten, as he said later, "every ache and pain and everything else."

"Burn the crutches," Mickey told his parents. "I'm going to play ball."

He was going to run hard the way the Cardinals' Enos Slaughter ran hard. Mickey wasn't going to worry any more about bone disease. If his ankle swelled up, well, he'd just bite his lip and bear the pain, and wait for the swelling to go down. And when it did go down, he'd get up and play again.

And that was the way it would always be for Mickey Mantle — the champion who should never have been. The disease would never go away and he would have to bite his lip and bear the pain and wait dozens of times in his career. And as soon as the swelling went down, Mickey would get up and play again.

Right after the 1946 World Series, Mickey and his dad sat down with pencil and paper. They drew up a master plan, charting Mickey's rise up through the minor leagues to the Yankees — the team that Mickey wanted to play for. By 1951, according to their plan, Mickey would be playing for one of the Yankees' Class A minor-league teams.

Mickey and his dad figured wrong. By

Mickey enjoys a card game at home with his family in 1951: Roy, Mickey, his mother, Larry, his father Mutt, and Ray.

1951 Mickey wouldn't be on a Class A minor-league team. He would be somewhere neither he nor his dad had dreamed of — in Yankee Stadium playing in a World Series!

That fall of 1946, despite his injured ankle, Mickey played halfback for the Commerce Tigers. He played so well that he was picked for the All-District team. In the winter he popped in long, two-handed set shots for the Commerce Tiger basketball team. And in the spring of 1947 he pitched and played shortstop for the Commerce Tiger baseball team.

Pitching in one game, Mickey struck out fourteen batters. In another game he hit one home run left-handed, then hit another home run right-handed. He was beginning to enjoy switch-hitting. And after a while pitchers refused to throw to Mickey. "When he came to the plate," his coach once said, "they'd walk him."

When the summer of 1947 rolled around, Mickey and Mutt had not forgotten about coach Barney Barnett's invitation to Mickey to join the Baxter Springs Whiz Kids. Barnett was the coach who had been impressed with Mickey's batting for the Miami team the year before.

"I know you got the big leagues figured

for him," Barney had told Mutt, "and I think you are figuring right. Maybe I can help."

Barney did help. He knew baseball and he knew boys. At the start of that 1947 season, Barney made Mickey the Whiz Kids' regular shortstop. Mickey still bobbled a lot of grounders hit straight at him. "You'll stay at shortstop," Barney told Mickey. "You don't quit on a ball even after you miss it."

At bat Mickey seldom missed. The Baxter Springs Whiz Kids played in a beautifully lighted park, but along the rear of the outfield, a river snaked its way. Any ball hit into this river would be an automatic home run. Since the river was some 400 feet from home plate, no one had ever belted a ball into the water.

One night Mickey jerked a pitch far over the right fielder's head. The ball rolled to the river's edge. Mickey circled the bases for an easy home run. In his next at-bat, Mickey ripped another drive over the outfielder's head, the ball again rolling to the edge of the river. Mickey ran around the bases for his second home run.

When Mickey came up the third time, Baxter Springs fans rose to their feet, screeching for a third home run. In came a fast ball. Mickey connected. The ball sped on a rising line toward center field. The center fielder ran straight back — right to the river's edge. There he stopped and watched the ball arc down — right into the middle of the river!

As Mickey jogged around the bases for the third time, the fans screamed their delight. They had seen Mickey put the first ball ever into the river.

After the game, fans passed around the hat; people dropped in whatever change they had. The money was dumped into Mickey's clubhouse locker — a total of $54. "I was ready to burst with happiness," Mickey wrote years later. "That was the largest amount of money I'd ever had all to myself at one time in all my young life. . . ."

That fall, though, the $54 almost finished Mickey in high school sports. He couldn't play football for the Commerce Tigers, school authorities said. By taking the $54 he had become a pro and could no longer play amateur sports.

Mickey couldn't believe that by accepting the money he had washed up his chance to participate in all high school sports.

He pleaded with the officials who finally said, "You can play if you return the $54." Of course the money was long spent. But

Mickey took jobs after school — jobs that paid as little as forty cents an hour. After many hours of work, he had the $54 and somehow got it back to all the fans who had contributed.

That year of 1947–48 was a busy one. Mickey played football in the fall, basketball that winter, baseball that spring. When summer came he rejoined the Whiz Kids.

Mickey was learning things about baseball that only the pros know. For example, he learned how to touch the bases on the inside when he was running out a double or a triple — cutting down the distance he had to run. He learned how to *charge* a ground ball instead of letting the grounder play *him*.

Almost by accident, he learned a tactic that would become a Mantle trademark: the drag bunt. This is how it came about. Long John Blair, a pitcher in the Gabby Street League, terrified batters with a whizzing fast ball. Few batters could hit him. Even Mickey had trouble. "This really ate into my soul," Mickey wrote in *The Education of a Baseball Player*, "because hitting was my pride."

Mickey decided he would bunt his way on base against Long John. When Long John fired his fast ball, Mickey stuck out his bat, making sure that he met the pitch with the fat part of the bat. Then, with his great speed, he dashed to first before Long John or a fielder could pick up the ball.

For years — in the Gabby Street League and in the big leagues — Mickey got many such drag-bunt singles. Because of Mickey's great power, the infielders had to play deep. But with his antelope speed, he could race to first in three seconds. And Mickey's deftness in placing his bunts made it pretty difficult for anyone to *get* to the ball in three seconds.

In the summer of 1948, Yankee scout Tom Greenwade came to Commerce. While he was there, a friend of his told him, "They got a kid playing for Baxter Springs. His name is Mickey Mantle."

"How good?" asked the lean, hatchet-faced Greenwade.

"Well," said his friend, "he plays shortstop. He makes a lot of errors. But he's got a big arm. He's terrifically fast on the bases. And he switch-hits as good right-handed as he does left-handed."

Greenwade went to see Mickey play. At the time, Mickey wasn't as big as other boys his age. After the game Greenwade told his friend: "He's kind of a bitty thing, not too much to see. But keep me posted on him."

That winter, Mickey's body suddenly filled out. His chest expanded, his arms thickened, his neck grew so that he wore a size 17 collar. By the spring of 1949, a few months before his high school graduation, Mickey had become a hefty 180-pound athlete.

In the spring, when Yankee scout Tom Greenwade came back to Commerce, he saw Mickey again. "The boy's grown," he said to Mutt Mantle.

"In more ways than one," Mutt answered. "The same thing happened to me when I was Mickey's age — I suddenly grew."

That evening Greenwade was in the stands with Mutt. Mickey knew the scout was watching his every move, and it made him nervous. He fumbled several grounders. But he also slammed a double, a triple, and a single in four times at bat.

Greenwade's face, as he watched Mickey, showed nothing of what he was thinking. Mutt was disappointed. He had expected the scout to be impressed and start talking about a Yankee contract. Especially after Mickey had connected for three hits. What did he expect Mickey to do anyway — hit four home runs in four at-bats?

"The Whiz Kids are playing Coffeyville again Sunday at Baxter Springs," Mutt said to Greenwade. "Maybe you ought to watch him then."

"I'll be there," said the scout. But there was no excitement in his voice.

The Mantle family was tense and nervous before the Sunday game with Coffeyville. Mutt Mantle had waited nearly eighteen years for a big-league scout to sign his son. Now, just when it seemed within grasp, were their hopes to be smashed?

The day before the game, Mickey practiced harder than ever. *He'd just better not make any errors this Sunday, that's all —* not with this big chance to play for his favorite team, the Yankees!

Then it was the night of the game. The smell of rain was in the air as the Whiz Kids ran onto the field. In the grandstand, Greenwade and Mutt Mantle watched the Whiz Kids' pitcher put down the Coffeyville hitters in order.

Now Mickey was striding to the plate. Mutt and Greenwade leaned forward expectantly. The pitcher threw. Mickey swung, drilling the ball on a line over the shortstop's head. Greenwade nodded.

The next two times up, Mickey hit a dou-

Scout Tom Greenwade grins as Mickey and Ralph Terry shake hands. Greenwade "took a chance" signing Mickey in 1949.

ble and a home run. Then rain, whipped by wind, poured down on the field.

The game was called and players and spectators ran to their cars. Mickey, his wet uniform flapping against cold skin, raced to his father's car. He flung open the door and jumped into the back seat. Mutt Mantle and Tom Greenwade were talking in the front.

"Well," said the scout, turning to Mickey, "I'm ready to sign you to a Yankee contract."

Greenwade continued talking in a low voice. He was taking a big chance, he said, in signing Mickey — he was still not big enough for the major leagues, he fielded badly, he had never hit tough pitching. "I can't offer you much of a bonus," Greenwade went on, "because, well — I don't think you're worth a bonus. But I'm willing to give you a Yankee check for $1,100 if you sign this contract, which will make you a member of the Independence ball club. You'll get paid about $140 a month until the end of the season."

Mickey looked at his father. Mutt nodded; the deal sounded all right to him. Mickey grinned his famous grin.

Their plan — and the hard work — had paid off!

4

Mickey Makes
the Big Club

MICKEY RAN OFF THE FIELD, his ears burn-
ing. *Another error!* How long could he
go on booting those ground balls?

He ducked into the dugout, head down,
looking like a kid who'd been scolded by his
teacher. Only he was not a kid — not any
more. He was a professional ballplayer now,
being paid to play baseball for a Yankee
farm team at Independence, Missouri, in this
1949 season.

Independence was in the Kansas-Okla-
homa-Missouri League. It was a Class D
league, the lowest in the minors, but Mickey
was a pro — as much of a pro as any big
leaguer.

Mickey was being paid good money too.
But how long would he be paid if he kept on
making errors?

"Mickey!" The worried, seventeen-year-old ballplayer looked up at the sound of his name. He saw his manager, Harry Craft, walking over to him.

"Look," barked Craft, "you'll never advance much higher than you are right now if you don't learn to keep your head up when you return to the dugout. You act as if you are ashamed of yourself. Yankees don't conduct themselves like that. Act like a champion."

Craft paused, staring at the red-faced young rookie. "Nobody is going to arrest you because you made an error. Look at the box scores tonight and you'll note that some of the big-league clubs committed more errors than we did."

Mickey did look at the scores, and it helped him recover some of his confidence. He realized that for every run he allowed with his sloppy fielding, he was batting in two with his lusty hitting. And soon the Independence team was far ahead of the rest of the clubs they played — teams like Carthage and Bartlesville.

The Independence team traveled in a big bus, and there was plenty of horseplay on board. When it got too wild, Craft would rise and shout, "Hold it." Immediately silence would descend over the entire bus. "I never knew a man quite like him for making his will known with a single stern glance," Mickey said later.

Mickey played 89 games for Independence and hit .313. He drove in 63 runs while scoring 54 — a good season for a rookie. But he did make 47 errors, an average of one every other game.

That winter, back home in Commerce, Mickey worked in the electrical shop of the Blue Goose Mine, making money for weekend dates. On one of those dates he met Merlyn Louise Johnson, a pert and pretty high school coed, and after several dates Merlyn became Mickey's steady girl friend. Merlyn's mother was amazed. She knew how shy Mickey was and how quiet Merlyn was. "I don't know how Merlyn and Mickey ever got acquainted," she said later. "Neither of them ever says a word."

In February 1950, Mickey took the train to Phoenix, Arizona. There the Yankees had set up an instructional camp for promising minor leaguers. In the camp the young players would get tips from Yankee players and coaches.

Riding to Phoenix, Mickey felt panic rising inside him. Last year he had played at Independence, only a few miles from home.

Now he was going to faraway Arizona. He'd miss his family — and Merlyn. And he'd be living and working among strangers. He was afraid he'd make a fool of himself and people would laugh at him.

On the first day at camp, Mickey walked toward the shortstop position. Standing nearby were Gil McDougald and Jerry Coleman — two Yankee stars. Mickey didn't dare take a position next to these famous men. Instead he stood on the outfield grass behind them. Whenever a ground ball scooted past them, Mickey would run over, pick it up, and toss it to one of them.

Soon Casey Stengel, then the Yankee manager, ambled out to talk to Mantle about playing shortstop. Mickey, ears red with shyness, couldn't even look at the manager. He stared down with embarrassment. "He kept looking at his feet," Stengel remembered later, "like they were going to fall off."

Mickey was too shy to make friends. That evening he went for a long walk by himself, while the other fifty rookies laughed and joked and got to know each other. Other evenings when they went to the movies, Mickey would sit alone in his room, writing letters, reading western stories, or brooding about home. Gradually, though, he came to feel more a part of the team. And incidents like the one that happened on his second day at camp helped:

Mickey was fielding grounders at shortstop when a slim, balding man in a Yankee uniform walked over to him. Mickey nodded. This man, he knew, was Frank Crosetti, now a Yankee coach and once a great shortstop for the Yankees.

Cro — as everyone called Crosetti — looked at Mickey's glove, a relic of Mickey's Whiz Kid days. It was scarred and battered. "Where did you get this?" Cro snapped. "You can't field a ball with that. Get yourself a decent glove."

Blushing, Mickey blurted out that he didn't have the money to buy a new glove. Cro shrugged and walked away.

The next morning Cro sauntered over to Mickey in the clubhouse and flipped a brand-new glove at him. Cro never told Mickey where he got the glove, but Mickey always had a hunch that the coach had bought it with his own money. The new glove helped Mickey cut down on his errors. But more important, Cro had helped Mickey to feel he belonged with the Yankees.

For the 1950 season, the Yankees graduated Mickey to Class C ball at Joplin, Mis-

UPI

For the Joplin, Missouri, farm team in 1950, Mickey batted
.383 and won the league's MVP award, but still fielded badly.

souri. Mickey was delighted. The manager at Joplin was the same Harry Craft who had taught him so much the year before in Independence. Mickey admired Craft almost as much as he admired Mutt Mantle.

Mickey still messed up balls hit right at him. Often he would flinch, turning his face as the ball shot toward him. If the ball took an unexpected hop, it often smacked him in the chin or chest, or simply scooted through his legs. "All in all," said Mickey years later, "I was a thorough-going butcher in the field."

But at bat he was a thorough-going terror. He hit .383 for Joplin, highest in the league, and he smacked 26 home runs. At the end of the season, writers voted Mickey the league's Most Valuable Player.

As Mickey stepped out of the dugout and walked toward home plate to receive the award, he felt very proud. And he knew that up in those stands, applauding with the crowd, was his father. Their plan was moving ahead more rapidly than they had hoped.

Near the end of the 1950 season, along with other minor leaguers, eighteen-year-old Mickey Mantle joined the regular Yankee club. He rode with the team on a western trip

— to Detroit, Cleveland, Chicago, and St. Louis — not playing, but getting a chance to take batting practice with the club. One day he stepped out of the batting cage after only two swings. "Take a few more swings, kid," yelled Joe DiMaggio. Mickey jumped back into the cage and took two more swings. That night he was still glowing over what had happened. The great Joe DiMaggio, his idol, had actually spoken to *him*.

At the end of the 1950 season Mutt Mantle, Merlyn, and Mickey's mother came to New York to watch the Yankees play the Phils in the World Series. Mickey introduced his father to some of the Yankees. He was proud of the casual way Mutt acted with these famous players. More than ever Mickey was sure of it: if his father had ever had the chance, he would have been a big-league player. One day he was listening to his father tell Phil Rizzuto how he had taught Mickey to switch-hit. Casey Stengel was also listening and said to Mutt, "Maybe I ought to sign *you* as a coach." Mickey smiled, pleased. His father would have been a great coach, he felt.

In February 1951, when Mickey again reported to the Yankee camp at Phoenix, he was no longer scared or homesick. He was nineteen years old, a guy who knew his way around. But he was still shy with strangers, and often when a reporter asked him a question, Mickey would stare blankly at the man, unable to think of an answer. Then Mickey would walk away, leaving the stunned reporter to conclude that Mantle was ignorant. He was far from ignorant, but with people he didn't know, his throat tightened when he tried to talk.

Mickey still brooded when he bobbled a grounder or threw a ball way over the first baseman's head. One day Casey Stengel was watching Mickey. "It isn't the wildness that bothers me," growled Casey. "He'll get over that once he isn't so nervous. But his hands aren't quick enough for a shortstop. He's lost if the ball takes a bad bounce."

On March 2, 1951, the Yankees heard a startling announcement: Joe DiMaggio, the great center fielder, announced he would retire at the end of the 1951 season. His legs ached almost constantly, and he wanted to quit while he was still near the peak of his skill.

The next day reporters saw coach Tommy Henrich hitting long fly balls to a young player in the outfield. "Who's that?" one of the reporters asked Henrich.

"Mickey Mantle," was the answer.

"What's he doing in the outfield? He's a shortstop, isn't he?"

"He's learning the outfield now," said Henrich. "Next year there's going to be a wide-open spot in center field."

Day after day Henrich coached Mickey in the art of playing the outfield — how to come in on drives, how to go back on long flies, how to throw to a base — even how to flip his sunglasses down. Mickey stumbled under pops, saw balls scoot through his legs, threw to the wrong bases.

One day Casey put Mickey into center field for a spring exhibition game. A batter hit a high fly. Mickey moved under the ball, and flipped down his sunglasses out of habit.

Black! Suddenly everything was black.

Thud! The ball smacked Mickey right on the nose. Right fielder Gene Woodling picked up the ball and threw it to the infield.

"What happened?" asked Woodling. Mickey mumbled something, trying to hide his embarrassment. He realized what had happened. The dark sunglasses, on this cloudy day, had blacked out his view of the ball!

As usual, though, Mickey made up for

his errors in the field by hitting the ball over fences. Near the end of spring training, Mickey owned a grand .402 batting average.

One day a reporter asked Casey what minor league Mickey would play in, in 1951. As usual Casey gave a rambling answer: "How do you pitch to him?" said Casey in his booming voice. "Right-handed? Left-handed? He can hit right-handed and he can hit left-handed.

"He's got to learn how to play the outfield. But his speed is so great that maybe he can use it in the outfield to make up for when he misjudges a ball. And his aim is so strong he can take a second to see where to throw the ball and still get it to the base in time to tag out a runner. He doesn't have to do it with instinct."

Casey frowned, thinking back to the original question: what would he do with Mickey? "All I know," said the manager, "is that he has me terribly confused and he's getting me more so every day. I know that he's not a big-league outfielder yet. He should have more minor-league ball under his belt. That's the only logical thing. But this kid isn't logical. He's a big-league hitter *now*."

Casey wasn't the only one impressed by Mickey's hitting feats. Writers poured praise

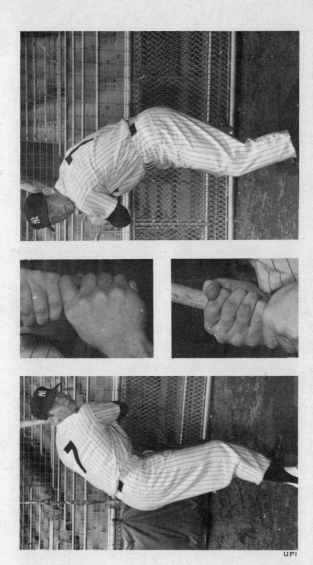

Mickey demonstrates his left- and right-handed batting stances and grips. His father forced him to learn to switch-hit.

on the rookie wonder. They described Mickey's powerful shoulders and muscular arms. They nicknamed him: The Commerce Comet, The Sweet Switcher.

One day Casey cut a number of rookies, sending them to Yankee minor-league camps. To Mickey's surprise, he *wasn't* cut. The Yankees broke camp at Phoenix and headed east for the opening game of the season in Washington. As the Yankee train whizzed eastward, Mickey thought about his future. Sure, he'd gotten a lot of publicity at camp. He knew that fans back in New York were talking about him, calling him a rookie sensation.

But what chance did he have of playing with the Yankees this year? Mickey felt he wasn't ready yet for the big leagues. He'd stayed with the Yankees longer this spring than he had expected. According to the plan drawn up by Mickey and his father, Mickey should be playing for a Class A team in 1951. That would be good enough for Mickey. The Yankees' Class A team that year was Beaumont, Texas. Mickey knew that Harry Craft, whom he had come to like so much, managed Beaumont.

Mickey had a thought: Should he ask Casey to send him to Beaumont? If he didn't ask, he might be sent to some other minor-league team. He'd miss not playing for Harry Craft.

Should he ask Casey now? Mickey gulped nervously. Casey might get mad at him and send him somewhere else. He braced himself and made a decision. Yes, he'd ask Casey right now.

Mickey walked down the aisle of the train to Casey's compartment. At the door he hesitated a moment, still very nervous. Then he knocked. Casey hollered, "Come on in." Mickey opened the door.

Casey looked up, surprised to see the shyest rookie of the team. Mickey tried to smile. He stammered something about being sorry to bother the manager. But he wondered, if, well, it might be possible for him to be sent down to Beaumont where the manager was Harry Craft and. . . .

Casey stared at him; his eyes seemed to look right through Mickey. Then Casey said, casually, "How'd you like to stay with the Yankees?"

5

Commerce Comet— or Flop?

MICKEY STILL COULDN'T BELIEVE IT: Casey Stengel had just asked him if he wanted to stick with the Yankees!

Mickey gulped once or twice and managed to say yes. Then Casey took him by the arm and led him to another compartment on the train to meet Yankee owner Dan Topping and general manager George Weiss. Quickly Mickey agreed to sign a contract for $7,000. "I'd have taken half that," Mickey admitted later on, "just to stay on with the big club."

The Yankees' opening game in Washington was washed out by rain. So the team went to New York for Opening Day at Yankee Stadium; the Yankees were playing the Boston Red Sox.

In the dugout, Mickey stared at a card

taped to the wall. Nine names were scrawled there:

Jackie Jensen LF
Phil Rizzuto SS
Mickey Mantle RF
Joe DiMaggio CF
Yogi Berra C
Johnny Mize 1B
Billy Johnson 3B
Jerry Coleman 2B
Vic Raschi P

Mickey read the batting order again, staring at his name. Then it really sunk in. He was batting in the third spot, right before his idol, Joe DiMaggio!

Mickey came out onto the green grass of Yankee Stadium and looked up at the towering triple-deck stands already filling up with spectators. He still could not believe his luck: he was really going to play today — in the big Opening Day of the 1951 season!

Just then Yogi Berra came up behind him. "Hey, what kind of an Opening Day is this?" growled Yogi. "There's no people here."

Mickey stared at Yogi, then realized that Yogi must have been joking. For Mickey had never seen so many people in one place in all his life.

Coach Jim Turner saw his glance. He tapped Mickey on the elbow. "How many people watched you play at Joplin last season?" he asked.

"I'd say about 55,000 all season," Mickey replied.

"Well, take a good look. We got about 45,-000 here today for one game — almost as many people as you saw in Joplin all year."

Mickey's jaw dropped open. "No!" he said.

"Yes," said Turner smiling, "and most of them came to see what you look like."

Turner was telling the truth. For weeks Yankee fans had been reading about the fabulous Mickey Mantle, the Commerce Comet. In the morning papers, sportswriters pointed out that Mickey was the first rookie in Yankee history to jump from a Class C team to the Yankees.

Mickey glanced over at the Red Sox dugout, where tall Ted Williams was swinging a bat. Mickey hoped Ted wouldn't hit a hard line drive at him in right field. He was so scared, a liner might knock the glove right off his hand.

Casey Stengel understood Mickey's fears.

As 1951 rookies, Mickey and the Giants' Willie Mays couldn't have guessed they would both become home-run champions.

"Last year he's a shortstop at Joplin," Casey told writers before the game. "Today he's in right field in Yankee Stadium." Casey looked at "the boy," as he called Mickey. "I'm praying for him," said Casey.

Suddenly it was game time. "Let's go," hollered Phil Rizzuto, the Yankee captain. The crowd roared a welcome as a wave of men in pin-striped uniforms swept onto the field.

Somehow Mickey got to right field. He thumped his glove nervously as Vic Raschi, the pitcher, stared down at the first hitter. Mickey hoped no one would hit a ball to him. No one did, as big Vic put down the Red Sox without a run.

Mickey ran in from right with that peculiar high-stepping gait of his acquired as a football halfback. In the dugout he selected a bat. Pitching for Boston was Bill Wight, a left-hander, so Mickey would be batting right-handed.

Minutes later Mickey walked toward the plate, his knees weak and wobbly. Wight twisted off a curve and Mickey swung.

Thwack! The bat splintered in half as the ball bounced across the grass toward second baseman Bobby Doerr. Bobby scooped up the ball and flipped it to first base.

Mickey flew down the base line. The ball smacked into the first baseman's mitt and a split second later Mickey's foot hit the bag. *Out!* signaled the umpire, fist flashing high into the air. But the crowd oohed its amazement. This kid was fast; he had come close to beating out an ordinary ground ball.

Then the Red Sox came to bat. First baseman Walt Dropo caught hold of a fast ball and hit a towering fly to right. Mickey started back, then saw the ball hanging white and high in the sky. He trotted in a few steps, tapping his glove. *Suppose he dropped an easy flyball in front of 45,000 people?*

Mickey settled under the ball, waited, caught it, and flipped it to Yankee second baseman Jerry Coleman. "Attaboy!" Jerry yelled at the rookie. Mickey's nervousness began to fade.

In his next at-bat, Mickey popped to the shortstop. Then, in the sixth inning, he came to the plate with runners on first and third and nobody out. Fans leaned forward; how would the kid do in the clutch?

Wight fired a humming fast ball. Mickey lashed at the pitch. *Crack!* It sounded good. Mickey dashed for first. Shortstop Johnny Pesky ran to his left, glove outstretched, to snare the ball. But it scooted by him into left field.

A base hit! Mickey's first big-league hit. And it had driven in a run.

Moments later Mickey came around to score on another base hit. As Mickey jumped into the Yankee dugout, DiMaggio and Rizzuto and other veterans slapped him on the back. "Good going, kid," they yelled. Mickey was really beginning to feel like a Yankee.

The Yanks won 5-0. The next day Mickey lined out another single, batting in two runs as the Yankees won again 6-3. A few days later Mickey rapped out three hits in five at-bats. Suddenly young Mickey Mantle, only nineteen years old, was a .320 hitter.

The club rolled west in a special Pullman car. After dinner some of the Yankees played cards. Mickey usually sat with the younger Yankees. But one evening Mickey saw that Rizzuto needed a player in his game. Mickey asked if he could play.

The small, wiry Rizzuto glared at Mickey. "I like your nerve," he yelled in a loud voice. The other Yankees turned to stare, grinning. Mickey's ears flamed red. "The idea of a busher like you asking to play cards with *me*," Rizzuto went on. "Son, you've got a lot to learn. Come back in a couple of years and

I might consider letting you *sit* next to me."

All the players were laughing. But it was a nightmare to a bashful person like Mickey. By now everyone in the car was staring at him.

Rizzuto sat down at a table. "Sit down, Mantle," he growled, "and let's play cards."

The other players roared with laughter. Mickey managed a weak grin. Rizzuto had been kidding him! Mickey sat down, his ears still red. But inside he was feeling good. Now he did really belong to this team of champions.

With reporters Mickey would still stare blankly when they asked him questions, too shy to express himself in words. But with the players he was losing his shyness — except with stars like DiMaggio, of whom he was still in awe.

In Chicago Mickey hit his first big-league home run — a 450-foot drive into the right-field stands.

Four days later, the Yankees came to Sportsman's Park in St. Louis to play the Browns. Watching from the stands — looking proud and trying not to show it — were Mickey's mother and his girl friend Merlyn. Mickey hit a home run. His mother and Merlyn stood and applauded. After the game

Mickey (number 6) steals second in this 1951 game. Before injuries weakened his knees, Mickey had tremendous speed. He didn't wear his now-famous number 7 until later that year.

a reporter asked Merlyn about the homer. "I expected it," she said simply. "He promised me he'd do it."

Mickey astounded the league with his power and speed. In a game at Detroit, Mickey was on first base when the batter bunted. The third baseman scooped up the ball and threw to first to retire the hitter. The first baseman cocked his arm to throw to second in case Mickey strayed too far from the bag.

But Mickey wasn't on second. He was running to third. The first baseman threw, but Mickey slid into third well ahead of the throw. "He went from first to third on a bunt!" said an amazed Stengel.

A few days later, in Cleveland, Mickey sliced a hit over the shortstop's head into left-center field. Cleveland center fielder Larry Doby ran over, picked up the ball, ready to throw to first base, and stared — mouth wide — as Mickey slid into *second*. "That's the first single I ever had to score as a double," a newsman said in the press box.

"You ain't seen nothing yet," Casey told writers, fracturing, as usual, the rules of grammar. "The kid doesn't run — he flies. He's positively the fastest man on the bases I've ever seen."

On other days, though, Casey grumbled because Mickey was striking out a lot — an average of once a game. He had a weakness for pitches up around his neck. Mickey couldn't resist going after those high pitches.

All those strikeouts began to pull down Mickey's batting average. Some fans began to think that Mantle was a one-month wonder. "In another month," said a New York writer, "Mantle the wonder will be Mantle the minor leaguer."

His average dipped below .290. In the first game of a double-header in Boston, Mickey struck out three times in a row before Stengel pulled him out of the game. Mickey started the second game and twice went down swinging.

He ran back to the dugout after that second strikeout, his head down, biting his lip. He was ashamed of himself. He had thought he was such a great hitter. Now all he could do was strike out.

Mickey hurled the bat angrily into the rack. Then he slumped down on the bench, dropping his head into his hands. And suddenly, right there in the dugout, he was crying. He said to Casey: "Put somebody in there who can hit the ball. I can't."

Casey nodded. "You go in for Mantle," he told reserve outfielder Cliff Mapes.

The next day Casey took Mickey aside. Mickey felt ashamed about crying in front of the other players. "Don't worry about that," the manager told Mickey. "You'll start for us when we get to Detroit."

But it was no better for Mickey in Detroit. Casey thought Mickey was a better hitter left-handed than right-handed. He tried to play Mickey only against righthanders so he would always bat left-handed. For a while, Mickey's average shot upward. But then he began to strike out again on those high pitches he couldn't resist.

On July 13, when the team arrived in Cleveland, Mickey's average was a weak .260. Casey had another idea. He would start Mickey in the lead-off position, hoping to take advantage of the youngster's speed on the bases.

But Mickey never got a base. Bob Lemon, the tough Cleveland pitcher, struck him out three times with high pitches — the pitch almost everyone was now throwing Mickey. The Yankees lost, and dropped two and a half games into second place.

After the game Mickey sat on a stool in the clubhouse, raging at himself. How could he stop striking out so often? He remembered how Long John Blair had struck him out so many times back in Oklahoma. He recalled what he had done then — he had bunted his way on base.

Mickey slammed fist against palm. That's what he'd do. In the next game in Detroit, on his first at-bat, he'd drag a bunt. He would get on base and start to lift his batting average. "I was as fast as anyone I had met in the majors," he said later on. "I knew that if I could not hit a pitcher, I could surely outrun him."

The next day, though, Casey called Mickey to his hotel room. Mickey walked in nervously, wondering what the manager was going to tell him.

Casey looked up at the boy. "Mickey," he said slowly, "you're getting a little nervous and tight at the plate, swinging at too many bad pitches. You're gonna develop into a big-league star one of these years. But maybe a change of scenery might do you a lot of good. I'm gonna send you to Kansas City. . . ."

He was being sent back to the minors! Mickey stared, trying to fight back tears. He was no longer a part of this Yankee team; he was a minor-league player again.

A few months earlier Mickey would have been delighted to go to Kansas City, at that time a triple-A team. But Mickey had come to feel a part of the regular team, a member of the world champion Yankees. He had heard the cheers of 50,000 people, felt the pride of wearing the Yankee pinstrips. Now all that was gone.

All the great things that had been predicted for him — a new Yankee superstar, another Joe DiMaggio — he had failed to accomplish. He was just another one-month wonder, a "phenom" who amazed everyone for a short while and then disappeared.

How disappointed his father would be! Mutt Mantle had waited all his life to see his son a big leaguer. Now Mickey had ruined that opportunity by striking out almost every other time he came to the plate.

Mickey left the hotel to go to the airport. "I was too choked up to tell anyone goodby," he said years later.

He was a flop, he told himself, a failure.

6

"What's the Matter, Kid?"

IN HIS HOTEL ROOM in Kansas City, Mickey
sat waiting for his father to come. He
was hoping Mutt would reassure him, tell
him he had nothing to be ashamed of. He'd
failed to become a big leaguer, of course,
but so do lots of people.

Mickey had been with the Kansas City
club for a week now — back with a minor-
league club after his brief run with the
Yankees.

In his first at-bat for Kansas City, he had
bunted his way on base. He'd felt better,
knowing he could still break out of a slump
by using his great speed to get on base. In
the dugout, though, his new manager, George
Selkirk, glared at him. "They didn't send
you down here to bunt!" Selkirk snapped.
"They sent you down here to hit."

Mickey turned, his face red, and ran to the outfield, his confidence squashed.

The next time he went to the plate Mickey swung feebly. He popped out, he grounded out, he struck out. In fact, in his next twenty-two at-bats, Mickey failed to get a hit.

So Mickey had written his dad that he wanted to go home. In Commerce he'd be among friends again, not moping around a hotel room. He'd work in the mines along with Mutt, and he'd save some money and marry Merlyn.

Oh, he'd play baseball on Sunday, just for the fun of it, and people would say, "That's Mickey Mantle. He played almost a half a season with the New York Yankees, and no one else from around here ever did that."

There was a knock on the door, and in walked Mutt. He was scowling and he didn't even shake hands. Instead, he just stared at Mickey. "If that's the way you are going to take this," Mutt Mantle said gruffly, "you don't belong in baseball anyway. If you have no more guts than that, just forget about the game completely. Come back and work in the mines, like me."

Mickey stood motionless, shocked. He looked at his shoes and muttered a promise.

All right, he'd try some more. He'd stay here in Kansas City. He wouldn't go home.

That night, as Mickey walked to the plate for his first at-bat, he was determined to make his father, watching from the stands, proud of him.

The pitch flashed toward the plate. Mickey swung and the ball arched high into the sky, climbing higher and higher. It dropped over a fence. As the crowd stood and cheered, Mickey circled the bases grinning. He knew that Mutt was up there grinning too.

Mickey came up again and clouted another home run. After the game his father came up to Mickey in the steamy clubhouse, and gave him the handshake Mickey had been waiting for. Mutt Mantle went back to Commerce — alone.

As Mickey said good-by, he noticed that his father looked much thinner. He had the "miseries" in his back, Mutt said, but he'd be all right soon.

As for Mickey, the miseries had vanished from his bat. After 40 games Mickey was hitting .361. He'd struck 11 home runs and driven in 50 runs.

Back in New York that summer, the Yankees were struggling to reach first place in the American League. In mid-August they hung in second place, three games behind the Indians.

Casey Stengel wanted help. On August 24 the Yankees recalled Mickey from the minors. Mickey raced to the airport and flew to Cleveland. He went straight to the ballpark and found Casey in the visitors' clubhouse. The night before, the Indians had beaten the Yankees 2-1. Casey needed hitting help. Was Mickey ready?

Mickey said yes, confidently, and trotted out to right field. That day the Yankees beat the Indians 2-0. The next day Mickey hit a long home run with a man on base, as the Yankees trampled Cleveland 7-3. Now Cleveland led by only a game.

The Yankees went on to St. Louis. Mutt Mantle came up from Commerce to see the game. He cheered as his son hit a single and a home run; the Yankees won two games. Now they were tied with Cleveland for the lead!

In New York the Yankees faced Washington. For six innings the Yanks' Eddie Lopat and Washington's Bob Porterfield retired batter after batter, locked in a scoreless tie. In the seventh Mickey came to the plate. With two men on base, Porterfield threw a fast ball. Mickey swung, driving the pitch on a rising line. The center fielder turned and ran. He raced to the bleacher wall, spun around, and watched the ball drop into the seats, more than 450 feet from home plate. It was one of the longest home runs ever hit at Yankee Stadium.

Eddie Lopat had all the runs he needed, and the Yanks won 4-0.

By mid-September the Yankees held first place, but by a thin margin; the Indians were hanging on. On the last week-end of the season, the Red Sox came to New York, opening with a double-header. If the Yankees could sweep both games of the double-header, they would win their fourth pennant in five years — and Mickey's first.

Mickey awoke that morning with a screech. His roommate, Johnny Hopp, had lashed a wet towel across his back. Then, as Mickey wiggled to escape that flailing towel, a glass of water was thrown in his face.

Mickey sputtered. Hank Bauer, his other roommate, was holding the empty glass and laughing. Grinning, Mickey got out of bed.

He was sharing an apartment on Broadway in New York City with Johnny Hopp and Hank Bauer. Mickey and Hank were especially good friends. The tough-looking ex-Marine was almost like a second father to Mickey. He showed this country boy how to order meals in fancy restaurants, and where to buy the right clothes. As a result, Mickey now looked like a man-about-town. Most important, perhaps, Hank had helped Mickey to overcome his shyness and make friends.

Mickey looked out the window as he dressed. It would be a good day for the game. Laughing, the three roommates went downstairs to breakfast at the Stage Delicatessen, a well-known midtown restaurant. Then they walked to the subway and took the D train north to the Bronx and Yankee Stadium.

To Mickey's chagrin, he wasn't in the starting line-up. Casey was going with his veterans to lock up the pennant. All through the first game Mickey sat on the bench, squirming. Still, it was a thrill to see the Big Chief, Allie Reynolds, pitch his second no-hitter of the season.

In the ninth inning, Allie was only three outs away from that second no-hitter. Mickey leaned forward, tense, as Allie got the first batter, then the second. And now Ted Williams, the Splendid Splinter, strode to the plate. Mickey knew the Big Chief wouldn't get his second no-hitter easily. He'd have to retire the league's best hitter first.

The count went to three balls and two strikes. The Stadium was hushed as Allie threw. Williams swung.

A pop foul! Right behind home plate. The Yankee catcher, Yogi Berra, circled under the ball, waiting, waiting. The ball arrowed down, hit his mit — and popped away.

The big crowd groaned. Embarrassed, Yogi snatched up his mask and trudged back to the plate. The Big Chief should have had his no-hitter. Instead he'd have to risk another pitch to Williams.

Mickey, standing now on the steps of the dugout, saw the stuff that champions are made of. Allie showed no disappointment, no anger, no self-pity. Calmly, he caught the ball thrown to him by the umpire. He stared down at Williams, ready to pitch again.

"In a tight situation," a champion will tell you, "you perform the way you always perform. You do nothing differently. You throw the way you always throw, you swing the way you always swing."

Now Allie pitched with the same motion he would use if this were a 10-0 game. Again Ted Williams lashed at the pitch.

Another pop foul! Yogi ran back toward

the screen. Again Mickey saw the stuff of champions. Circling under the ball, knowing he would be laughed at across a nation if he should drop *this* foul, Yogi waited. Then he settled under the ball, held the mitt close to his chest, and squeezed the ball. The Yankees could be sure of at least a tie for the pennant.

And in the second game the Yankees clinched the pennant. In the sixth inning of that game, Joe DiMaggio hit his 361st home run. When Mickey reached over to pump Joe's hand later, in the dugout, neither man could know that this would be DiMaggio's last home run in a regular-season game, or that the rookie shaking his hand would take over as the next great Yankee center fielder.

On the last out, Mickey rushed onto the field with the other Yankees to congratulate the winning pitcher, Vic Raschi. In his first year in the big leagues, Mickey was with a winning team. And he had helped to win that pennant. He had played in 96 games and batted in 65 runs while scoring 61. Of his 91 hits, 13 were home runs, 5 were triples, and 11 were doubles. His batting average, .267, was a good one for a kid just up from Class C.

A few days after the Yankees clinched the

American League pennant, the Giants and Dodgers fought a three-game play-off to win the right to oppose the Yankees. Mutt Mantle came to New York to see that play-off, and the Series. He was at the Polo Grounds for the final game of the play-off. The Giants were behind 4-2, with two men on base in the ninth. Then Bobby Thomson hit his historic home run, a line drive into the left-field seats that gave the National League pennant to the Giants.

That evening Mutt told Mickey how excited he had been watching Thomson's home run. Mickey glanced at his father as he nodded. Mutt didn't look well, he thought. He was thin and pale. Mickey began to worry that his dad might be sicker than he had let on.

The day after Thomson's home run, the World Series opened in Yankee Stadium between the pennant teams. Mickey woke up feeling nervous, "ten times tighter than I was when I played my first big-league game," he said later.

He and his father took an early-morning ride up Fifth Avenue, staring at the tall office buildings and the plush store windows. The ride calmed Mickey down. At the Stadium he said to Mutt, "I'm as loose as saw-dust."

But the Giants' Dave Koslo turned the Yankee bats to sawdust in the first game, beating their cross-town rivals 5-1. And the Yanks' lead-off man, Mickey Mantle, failed to get a hit.

Mickey led off the second game with a drag-bunt single. He came around to score and the Yankees took a 1-0 lead.

In the fifth inning, another much-heralded rookie — Willie Mays — stepped up to the plate for the Giants. He too had played part of the 1951 season in the minors. Now he roamed center field for the Giants and hit with power to all fields. Mickey edged back a few feet in right field.

In came the pitch. Mays swung and rammed a high line drive toward right-center field. Mickey dashed to his right for the ball.

Suddenly — just like that — he fell to the ground and lay there. Joe DiMaggio swooped in behind Mickey and caught the ball. Then he bent over the stricken rookie.

"What's the matter, kid?" he said, bewildered.

Mickey started to mumble something and then fainted. The Yankees carried Mickey

In the 1951 World Series, Mickey suddenly collapses. Joe Di-Maggio catches the ball, then asks, "What's the matter, kid?"

off the field on a stretcher. In the clubhouse Mickey came to. What had happened?

He said he didn't know. He'd been running and then he heard a loud snap and went down.

A trainer said he thought Mickey had stepped into a drainage hole. "I may have run over that hole," said Mickey. "But I just don't know. All I know is that one second I was running and the next second my knee was giving out. I fell and stayed on the ground. I was really scared."

In the clubhouse Mickey stared at the injured knee. He'd hurt the right one — his good knee. It was his left knee that had been weakened by osteomyelitis.

A little later the Yankees flocked into the clubhouse. They'd won the game 3-1. After dressing, Mickey limped out of the Stadium and went back to his hotel.

The next morning, Mutt Mantle, Mickey, and the doctor took a cab to Lenox Hill Hospital where Mickey's knee was to be X-rayed. As Mickey got out of the cab, he leaned on his father for support — and Mutt fell to the ground. The doctor saw that he now had two patients.

Doctors X-rayed Mickey's knee. "There's a torn ligament on the inner side of the leg," they told Mickey. "You'll be watching the rest of the Series on a television set in a hospital room, but the knee should be all right by next spring."

That evening Mickey rested the knee in a hospital bed and in a bed next to him lay his father looking thinner than ever. "My back's acting up again," he told Mickey. "The rest might do me some good. Besides I've got to watch that knee of yours."

Mickey grinned. But he didn't believe it. Something was wrong — very wrong — with Mutt Mantle.

7

Boos for Mickey

WHAT MICKEY HALF GUESSED and dreaded
was true: Mutt Mantle was very sick. He
had cancer and he was dying. Toward the
end Mutt went out to Denver, so that his
family would not have to watch him waste
away.

Mickey's father died in May. The evening
of the day that Mickey heard the news he
was scheduled to play a night game in Yankee Stadium, and Mickey played that game.
"I knew Dad would have wanted me to
play," he said.

In his book, *The Quality of Courage*, Mickey called his father "the bravest man I ever
knew . . . he never complained, he never
acted scared. . . ." And whenever Mickey
talked about the people who had made him a
big-league star, the first man he mentioned

was the one who had been his first baseball coach — Mutt Mantle.

Mickey went to Oklahoma to attend his father's funeral. He returned with a firm resolve: to really make good in the big leagues. And he really had to. For baseball now was no longer just a game. It was a job, the only way Mickey knew of making a living. And Mickey needed a good job. He was supporting his mother, his younger brothers and sister — and his new wife, Merlyn, whom he had married the previous winter.

Early in the 1952 season, though, Mickey was playing the game at half-speed. That winter he had injured his right knee again, playing basketball. All through spring training, Mickey limped after flyballs. Casey had planned to use Mickey to replace the retired Joe DiMaggio. But now Mickey was too slow to cover the entire center field.

So Mickey played right field. One day he was slow in reaching a fly into right center. He lunged for it, sticking out his glove. The ball hit the glove and bounced up, hitting Mickey right between the eyes. "I was so ashamed," said Mickey years later. "I wanted to die right there."

Stengel tried Jackie Jensen, Bob Cerv, and Irv Noren in center field. None of them won the job. Then Casey moved Mickey from right field to third base. In his one game at third, Mickey muffed two grounders in four tries.

The next day Mickey was playing the bench. He stayed on the bench for four games, while Casey desperately juggled his outfielders, trying to find a winning combination.

Then the Yankees came to Chicago for a series with the White Sox. To his surprise, Mickey saw on the line-up card that he was playing center field, and batting third.

In his first at-bat, Mickey cracked a single. As he sprinted to first, his right knee suddenly felt strong again; the ache was gone. When the inning ended, Mickey grabbed his glove and ran confidently to center field. He knew he could catch any ball now.

That day he slammed four hits in four at-bats. The four hits jumped his average to .315. Casey, watching from the dugout, knew he'd found himself a center fielder at last.

Casey was famous for platooning players. At first base, for instance, he might play a left-handed hitter when the Yankees were facing a righty pitcher, then a right-handed hitter if the Yankees were facing a lefty pitcher. These players were platoon players. A few players — Phil Rizzuto at shortstop, Yogi Berra behind the plate — played every day. They were regulars.

Right from the start Mickey was a regular. Casey did not platoon him at all after that game in Chicago in 1952.

As Casey put it, "That boy can run too fast and hit that ball too far over those fences for him to be sitting on a bench during seventy games a season. I got to have him in my line-up every day."

In a double-header that July, Mickey smacked a long home run batting right-handed, then came up in the second game batting left-handed, and hit another long home run. The Yankees won both games, forging into first place.

But late in July they dropped six out of seven games. The White Sox came to New York, and in the first game of their series jumped into a 7-0 lead. They were still ahead 7-0 in the bottom half of the seventh, their ace lefthander, Billy Pierce, breezing along.

Mickey came to the plate with a runner on base. He smacked a long double, scoring the runner. Moments later, Mickey scored.

The Yankees picked up another run and now trailed 7-3.

Unruffled, Pierce stopped the Yankees in the eighth and went into the last of the ninth still ahead 7-3. Then the Yankees exploded hits, and suddenly the score was 7-6.

With the bases loaded and two out, Mickey came up to bat. Chuck Stobbs of the White Sox, a hard-throwing veteran, had replaced Pierce. He zipped a fast ball at Mickey. *Crack!* The ball rocketed down the left-field line. Back went the left fielder to the wall. He turned and stretched his glove. But the ball arched over his fingertips and dropped into the seats.

Home run, a grand-slam home run! The Yankees had won 10-7. The players crowded around Mickey. Thanks to him they were feeling like champions again.

That rally snapped life back into the Yankees. By early September they held a three-and-a-half-game lead. Then the Indians made a stretch run at the Yankees. On September 21 the Yankees walked into Cleveland's Municipal Stadium, ahead by only a game and a half. Some 73,000 Cleveland fans squeezed into the big ball park, roaring for a victory.

In the first inning Mickey doubled, and

the Yankees had an early lead. In the fifth he hit a home run that put them comfortably ahead and the Yankees coasted to victory. When they left Cleveland they were two and a half games in front.

In Boston, with the score tied in the tenth, Mickey hit a triple to give the Yankees a 3-2 triumph. In another game against Boston, Mickey hit a single, a triple, and a home run, driving in four runs as the Yankees won another precious game 8-6.

On the night of September 26 against the Philadelphia A's, Mickey rapped out a long home run to seal a 5-2 Yankee victory. It clinched the pennant for the Yankees. In the clubhouse celebration afterward, Mickey joked and laughed as hard as anyone. Unlike last year, when he had watched from the bench, Mickey had played in this pennant-clincher and helped to win it. Mickey's .311 batting average was the third highest in the American League. He had hit 23 home runs, driving in 87 runs. In only his fourth season of professional baseball, Mickey had become a big-league star.

But he knew he still had to polish his fielding. He had made fourteen errors, more than any outfielder in the league. "Line drives straight at me are still trouble," he admitted.

"I can't tell if a ball's hit real good or if it is going to drop in front of me."

That year Mickey and Larry Doby of the Indians had each struck out 111 times. "Anybody swings as hard as Mickey or me is going to strike out a lot," Doby told a reporter. "It's natural for him to swing hard and he always will."

As the 1952 season ended, Mickey was looking forward to the World Series — this time against the Dodgers, then in Brooklyn. Experts called this team one of the National League's all-time best. It boasted stars like PeeWee Reese at shortstop, Jackie Robinson at second, Roy Campanella behind the plate, Duke Snider in center field, Carl Furillo in right field, and on the mound Don Newcombe, Preacher Roe, and Joe Black.

Mickey wasn't as nervous before this Series as he had been the year before against the Giants. He respected the great Brooklyn pitchers, but he knew now what he could do. He wasn't afraid to walk out there and swing. He had confidence he would get his share of hits.

In the first game he cracked two singles against Joe Black but the Yankees lost 4-2. In the second game Mickey knocked a double and two singles, and the Yankees won.

The Dodgers took the third game, the only game in this Series in which they would stop Mickey without a hit. The Yankees won the fourth game 2-0, Mickey slamming a triple to score one of the Yankee runs.

The Dodgers moved ahead, three games to two, by winning the fifth game. Now the Yankees stood at the edge of defeat. If they lost once more they fell as world champions. They *had* to win the next two games.

In the eighth inning of the sixth game, the Yankees led 2-1. Mickey came up to the plate and hit a long home run to make the score 3-1. That home run proved decisive, because Duke Snider came up in the bottom of the eighth with a home run that would have tied the score. Instead the Yanks won 3-2.

Now the two teams faced each other for the seventh and final game. Dodger fans crammed into Brooklyn's old Ebbets Field and screeched for victory. Joe Black was pitching for Brooklyn; Eddie Lopat was throwing his tricky stuff for the Yankees.

The two teams went into the sixth inning tied 2-2. Mickey came up to bat. He hooked into a fast ball and hammered it high over the towering right-field wall. The Yankees led 3-2.

A little later Mickey came to the plate

against Preacher Roe. He knocked a line-drive single into left field, driving home another run. That was the ball game. The Yankees had won 4-2.

In the gloom of the loser's clubhouse, Jackie Robinson said what all the Dodgers were thinking: "Mantle beat us," he said. "Who would have thought the Yankees could lose a great star like DiMaggio and right away find someone to replace him? Against us he was every bit as great as Joe DiMaggio."

In the winner's clubhouse, his blond hair mussed, stood twenty-year-old Mickey Mantle, the hero of the Series. Writers threw questions at him, and this time he answered them all, grinning, photographers' flash bulbs lighting up his face.

When Mickey went home to Commerce afterward, almost 7,500 people — three times the town's population — jammed the streets to cheer him. Mickey and Merlyn rode in the back seat of an open car, waving to the crowd. A brass band blared, drum majorettes and signs proclaimed what Commerce thought of "Our Hero, Mickey Mantle."

That night Mickey attended a banquet in his honor. His boyhood pals, teachers he had

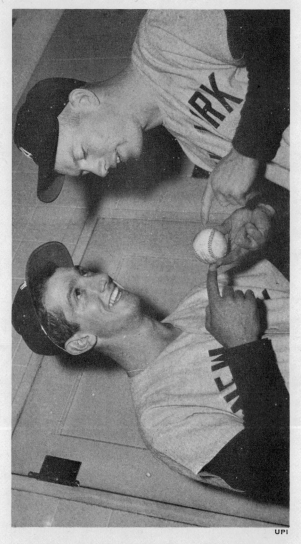

In 1953 Mickey holds the ball he blasted out of Washington's
Griffith Stadium. Here his close friend Billy Martin looks on.

known — almost everyone who knew Mickey — were there. They stood and cheered. Mickey raised his hands and in the quiet that followed, he said simply, "Thanks, everybody."

During the winter of 1952-53, people in baseball talked about the future of baseball's newest superstar. Said Casey Stengel, "He has more left-handed power than anyone except Babe Ruth, more right-handed power than anyone except Jimmy Foxx."

At the start of the 1953 season, fans filled baseball parks to see this newest wonder. In Washington Mickey showed just how much power he had. Swinging right-handed, he belted a tremendous home run. Someone measured the distance at 565 feet. "I don't care how far it went," said Stengel. "It was the longest ball I ever saw get hit." Stengel spoke from forty years' experience.

By July Mickey led the league in hitting with a .350 average. He was picked as the American League's All-Star center fielder for the All-Star game. But in August Mickey wrenched a knee. As Mickey limped through the rest of the season, his hitting suffered. He finished with a .295 average, 21 home runs, and 92 runs batted in.

It had been a good year. But this was

Mickey Mantle — the player who was supposed to be another DiMaggio, another Ruth, another Jimmy Foxx. Fans expected more of him than a .295 average and 21 home runs.

In New York fans began to boo Mickey — especially when he struck out. In the 1953 Series the Yankees again beat Brooklyn. Mickey won two games with clutch home runs, but he struck out eight times, once fanning four times in a row.

By 1954 the boos for Mantle were as much a part of Yankee Stadium as home plate. The Yankees won 103 games that season, but the Indians won 111 and the pennant. Mickey had a fine year, hitting .300, 27 home runs and scoring 129 runs, the most in the league.

And yet the fans continued to boo Mickey. They talked of the greatness of DiMaggio. They raved about the brilliance of two other New York center fielders — Willie Mays of the Giants, and Duke Snider of the Dodgers. They sneered at Mantle's "tape-measure" jobs, as sportswriters had christened his long home runs.

In 1955 Mickey changed his batting stance. He was determined to cut down on his strikeouts. That year he struck out only

81 times — his lowest total ever. What's more, he hit 37 home runs, the most in the American League. And he made only two errors in the outfield.

Mickey's fielding improved greatly. The one-time shortstop became a spectacular outfielder. He raced after long drives to catch the ball over his shoulder like a football end. He charged in to pick balls off the grass at his shoetops. He threw out runners with line-drive throws from center field to home plate. But it didn't matter. Yankee fans refused to be impressed by anything Mickey did.

"The balls Mantle catches with those long runs," they said, "DiMaggio or Mays or Snider would catch easily. Mays and Snider don't misjudge flies the way Mantle does."

The boos that continued to roll down from the stands enraged Casey. "He doesn't have to strike out any more to get booed," said the manager. "Even when he hits a home run, they boo him. He can do more things better than anybody in baseball and still they boo him. It's not right."

Even the sportswriters were beginning to scorn Mickey. They wrote about how great he was supposed to have been — the Commerce Comet, the Switcher, another Ruth, another DiMaggio. "The fact remains," wrote one reporter, "that he is not the ballplayer he has been expected to be. Nor is it certain that he will ever reach that hoped-for pinnacle."

Fans and writers had set certain goals for Mickey. He hadn't reached those goals, so they abused him in print, booed him in the ballparks.

Naturally, Mickey heard the boos and they hurt him. "I'm not complaining," he told a friend. "Ballplayers have no right to complain about the fans booing. But it sure makes me feel better when they cheer."

His unpopularity worried him a lot. Why didn't Yankee fans like him? What could he do to make them like him?

8

The Change in Mantle

IN THE SPRING OF 1956 a young sportswriter stood waiting for a taxi to take him to Miller Huggins Field at St. Petersburg, Florida. He had made an appointment to interview Mickey Mantle for a magazine, and he didn't want to be late. He was afraid Mickey might use it as an excuse not to speak to him at all, for the writer had heard stories about Mickey's shyness, how he hated to talk about himself, especially to people he didn't know.

Suddenly, the writer saw a car speeding toward him — not a taxi but a convertible. And Mickey was at the wheel! Mickey waved and skidded to a stop. "Get in," he said. "I'll drive you to the park."

Although he didn't have much to say during the twenty-minute ride to the Yankees' training headquarters, Mickey was friendly, and he did most of the talking in his interview in the clubhouse later. He discussed his father, the decision he had made in the Kansas City hotel room five years before to go on playing, and his batting technique.

"When I swing right-handed I get more power. That's because my swing is more level. When I swing left-handed, I cut up at the ball, I strike out more often, and I don't get as much power on the ball. But I get a lot more singles batting left-handed than right-handed."

The writer was amazed. Was this the Mantle no one could get to talk?

That afternoon another reporter was watching a group of young Yankees taking hitting practice. He realized that Mickey was standing next to him. All at once, Mickey started talking to him. "We've got some promising kids on this squad," he said, and then he named a few. Mickey had volunteered information without being asked! That evening the reporter told his newspaper readers that, "Mantle for the first time has ceased to regard himself as a kid, and is taking on the status of an old hand and liking it."

Mickey *was* getting older, more mature. He was twenty-four now and growing more confident. He'd been in the big leagues for five years and he was getting accustomed to the quick questions thrown at him by reporters, the clamor of the fans for autographs.

Something else had brought about the change in Mickey's attitude toward the public. It had begun the previous winter.

Shortly after he signed his 1956 contract — for $30,000, the most the Yankees had paid him up to that time — Mickey had a talk with Bill DeWitt. This Yankee official had been in baseball more than thirty years, and he talked straight with Mickey about those boos he was getting at the Stadium. True, Mickey was still one of the newer players, and newcomers are usually booed more often. Also, he'd taken over from one of baseball's best-loved players, DiMaggio, whose fans may have resented Mantle. Added to all this, Mickey's performance was uneven because he played so often in pain. Still . . .

"Maybe a ballplayer has to do more than have a good season on the field," DeWitt told Mickey. "Maybe he has to win a little personal popularity."

Mickey had to come out of his shell, DeWitt said. He had to let New York fans know that he cared, that he didn't like to be

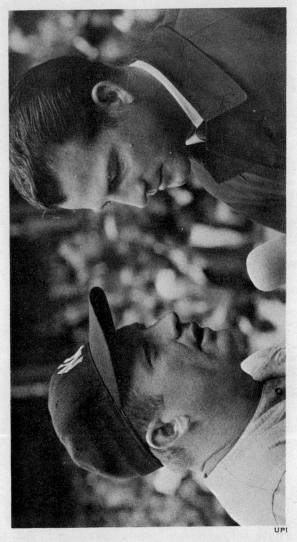

UPI

With great difficulty, Mickey overcame his shyness with reporters. Here he talks with sportcaster Frank Gifford.

booed, that he wanted praise and applause as much as anyone. Mickey was a warm and witty human being whom the younger Yankees looked up to with awe, but the fans didn't know that. When they found out the kind of person Mickey really was, DeWitt said, the booing would stop. But Mickey *had* to break out of his shell of shyness.

So that spring Mickey really made an effort. He talked more with reporters, he gave interviews, and he tried to do things for people that he simply had never thought about doing before.

Mickey was famous now, and fame is a wonderful thing. But there is a price for it — for instance, having to sign hundreds of autographs at a time, or having to drive a hundred miles after a tough game to make a speech. Mickey was learning to pay the price for fame.

He was also learning — during this spring of 1956 — how to hit fast balls close to his belt. In a game against the Cardinals in St. Petersburg, Mickey drove a pitch over the right-field fence. Stan Musial, playing right field for the Cardinals, turned to watch the ball soar into the street. "No home run ever cleared my head by so much as long as I can remember," Stan said after the game. "The kid looks different this year. He always struck out a lot but now he's letting bad pitches go. If he hits sixty homers and bats .400, I can't say I'll be surprised."

That same spring of 1956 an Associated Press writer, Joe Reichler, suggested that Mickey might win one of baseball's most coveted prizes — the Triple Crown. The three crowns are the batting championship, the home run championship, and the runs-batted-in championship. No one had won the Triple Crown since Ted Williams in 1947. And only eight men had ever won the Triple Crown in the history of baseball. They were Ty Cobb, Henry Zimmerman, Rogers Hornsby, Chuck Klein, Jimmy Foxx, Lou Gehrig, Joe Medwick, and Ted Williams.

Could Mickey match the record of such all-time greats as Cobb and Williams?

Reporters asked Casey Stengel about it. He had played big-league ball in Cobb's time. "How can I say what the kid will do?" Casey said, his voice booming through the clubhouse. "Who can say Mantle will be *playing* tomorrow? Or the day after tomorrow? He's got those bad legs. How can I say what a kid will do who may fall down tomorrow and never play again?"

Never play again! Each time Mickey

walked out onto a ballfield, bandages wrapped around his knees, he knew he might be carried off — never to play again. He had been rejected by the United States Army because of his bad left leg. It could collapse under him at any time, even on a battlefield — or on a ballfield — and Mickey knew it.

Besides having osteomyelitis, Mickey was more injury prone than most ballplayers. Already in the 1951 World Series he'd torn ligaments in the right knee. Three years later a cyst had to be cut from that knee. In 1955 he'd pulled a thigh muscle. And many more injuries were to follow.

Ten days before the 1956 season, Mickey bruised a leg, sliding. But Mickey had learned how to play in pain. He was in the starting line-up for Opening Day in Washington against the Senators.

In his first at-bat Mickey drove a curve ball into the center-field seats, 450 feet from home plate. In the sixth he slugged another "tape-measure job" — the sportswriters' name for his long home runs.

The Yankees came to New York and Mickey hit another home run in Yankee Stadium. The next day he hit another. And suddenly people were talking about whether

Mickey could break Babe Ruth's record of sixty home runs in a season.

On Memorial Day Mickey came to bat against the Senators' Pedro Ramos. He swung at a fast ball, bunching all his strength into the swing.

The ball rose toward the towering, triple-deck, right-field stands like a soaring white gull. Higher and higher it rose. No one — not even Ruth — had ever hit a fair ball out of Yankee Stadium. Would this ball clear the roof?

It didn't — not quite. It hit the facade two feet below the roof, then dropped a hundred feet to the lower stands. But no one had come as close to hitting a homer out of the Stadium.

In the clubhouse after the game, reporters clustered around Mickey. "Where do you get all that strength?" they asked. The slugger shrugged, grinning.

Mickey is six feet and weighs about 195 pounds. Many players are taller and heavier, but few match his compact strength. He has the barrel chest and bulging arms of a pro wrestler; the thick legs and strong, seventeen-inch neck of a football guard. "He is the strongest guy on this team," a Yankee once told a reporter. "He may be the strongest man alive."

By June Mickey had hit twenty-one homers. His batting average stood at .407. In every town where the Yankees played, they saw the same headline: *Can Mickey Break Ruth's Record?*

"You know, this is quite a strain," his friend, Yankee right fielder Hank Bauer, said. "Everywhere Mickey goes, he is asked if he thinks he can break Ruth's record. I must say he takes it all right. He's not scared of people anymore. He's really grown up all of a sudden."

"I'm not much at talking," Mickey conceded in the clubhouse. "I never have a great deal to say. Some people think I'm not friendly because of that. I wish I *could* act more friendly."

Mickey may not have realized this, but that speech showed how much he had changed. A year or two earlier he would never have found the words to tell a stranger that he wished he could be more friendly. And as a result, sportswriters and their readers were beginning to really like and appreciate Mickey Mantle.

On August 11 a Baltimore pitcher threw a low pitch. Mickey jerked the ball off his shoelaces and slammed it into the upper deck. As Mickey rounded the bases, applause filled the Stadium. The next time Mickey came to bat, he heard the usual boos. Not as many, though. A lot more people were cheering than booing Mantle. More and more fans agreed with Baltimore manager Paul Richards: "Mantle can hit better than anyone else, field better than anyone else, he can throw better, and he can run better. What else is there? Mantle is a super player."

At the start of September Mickey needed fourteen home runs to break Ruth's record. He knew he wasn't likely to hit that many in the few games remaining, so he set his sights on another goal — the Triple Crown.

He led the league in home runs, in batting, in runs batted-in. He knew he would win the home-run race; with 47 he was far ahead. But Ted Williams was only a few points behind him in batting, and Detroit's Al Kaline trailed Mickey by only a few RBI's.

Mickey decided he'd swing mostly for singles and doubles. They would keep his average high and help him drive in more runs.

But suddenly Mickey was swinging for outs; in thinking so hard about the Triple

Crown, he had tightened at the plate. "You're lunging at the ball instead of swinging at it," Casey told him. Mickey stopped lunging, and the hits began to fall in again.

The Yankees, meanwhile, romped toward their second straight pennant — their fifth in the six years Mickey had been a Yankee. On the night of September 18, Mickey hit an eleventh-inning home run to beat the White Sox and clinch the American League pennant.

Now the big race in the American League was for the Triple Crown. With only three days left in the 1956 season, Mickey led Williams in batting, .354 to .348. In the RBI department, Mickey led Kaline, 127 to 124.

In the next-to-final game of the season, Mickey singled, driving in his 129th run. Ted Williams had a poor day, and that single clinched the batting title for Mickey. But Al Kaline had a marvelous day at the plate and suddenly he had 128 RBI's, only one fewer than Mickey.

The next day was the final day of the season. In that final game, Mickey drove in his 130th run. But in Detroit the Tiger game was still going on. How was Kaline doing? If he could drive in three runs, he would wrest that RBI title away from Mickey.

After the game Mickey dressed quickly in the clubhouse and rushed downtown to the apartment he now shared with Yankee infielder Billy Martin. As soon as he opened the door he heard excited voices: the news from Detroit was that Kaline had failed to drive in a run!

Mickey had hit 52 home runs and driven in 130 runs. He had hit .353.

He had won the Triple Crown!

In the World Series the Yankees went to bat against an old foe — the Dodgers. Mickey hit three home runs in that series, he drove in four runs, he scored six. And again the Yankees won in seven games. So far Mickey had played in five World Series, and the Yankees had won four of them, losing only to the Dodgers in 1955.

A few weeks after the Series, the nation's sportswriters named Mickey the American League's Most Valuable Player.

That winter Mickey attended a banquet in Chicago. The guest of honor was Casey Stengel. Before the banquet Mickey said to Bob Fishel, the Yankees' publicity man, "I wouldn't mind getting up there and saying a few words about Casey."

That evening the toastmaster asked Mickey to say those few words. Mickey talked

The great Yankee manager Casey Stengel and Mickey pose
for photographers after Mickey won the Triple Crown in 1956.

for fifteen minutes about Casey and how he had helped him as a ballplayer. When Mickey finished, the crowd stood up and applauded.

In that crowd was Bill DeWitt. "The change in the boy is fantastic," he said. "I have never seen anyone gain so much confidence in so short a time. A year ago, the very idea of making a speech would have terrified him. He certainly wouldn't have *volunteered* to stand up and talk."

Mickey was doing everything he could to turn boos into cheers.

9

M & M
(Maris and Mantle)

IN JUNE OF THE 1960 SEASON Mickey was batting .225. He knew he wasn't doing well. A lot of fans, especially younger ones, were cheering him, but Mickey could still hear some booing.

Yet he had done great things since the 1956 season, when he had won the Triple Crown and first made a real attempt to meet the reporters.

In 1957 he hit .365 and 34 home runs to win his second straight Most Valuable Player Award. True, that year the Braves had beaten the Yankees in the Series. But significantly, Mickey had missed much of that Series after injuring his shoulder in a collision at second base. It was then that the feeling began to grow in the Yankee dugout: we need Mickey in the line-up to win.

In 1958 Mickey's shoulder ached most of

the season. But the pain didn't stop him from rapping out 42 home runs to lead the league. He batted .304 as the Yankees won their fourth straight pennant — the seventh they had won in the eight years that Mickey had been a Yankee. In that 1958 Series the Yankees met the Braves again. They were down, three games to one. This time Mickey played all the way, and the Yankees roared back to win the final three games and the world championship.

In 1959 Mickey hit .285 and 31 homers — a grand year for anyone — anyone but Mickey Mantle. The booing grew louder that year as the Yankees slipped at the start and finished fifteen games behind the pennant-winning White Sox.

Now, in 1960, Mickey and the team were starting slowly again. By August Mickey had raised his average and the team was in contention, only a few games behind the leaders. But Mickey was bothered. He knew he should be doing better for the team. Knowing that, his anger flared — anger at himself for *not* doing better.

One day in August Mickey came to the plate against the Senators. The Yankees were losing 3–2. Roger Maris, a new out-fielder the Yankees had obtained from the

Kansas City A's, stood on first base. Mickey reminded himself that there were two outs. A home run, he knew, would put the Yankees ahead.

In came the pitch. Mickey swung and hit an easy hopper right at the third baseman. An easy third out. Mickey knew the third baseman would flip the ball to second for a forceout. He ran slowly toward first as he mentally berated himself. Why *wasn't* he doing better?

Then Mickey heard the crowd burst into a roar. He looked toward second base. Maris had slid hard into second, trying to knock down the second baseman. But the second baseman had hopped over the sliding Maris and was shooting the ball toward first.

There must have been only one out! Mickey jerked into high speed, running to beat that double-play throw to first. But Mickey was yards from the bag when the ball thudded into the first baseman's mitt. He had hit into a double play, the inning was over, the Yankee rally was ended.

Mickey ran, crimson-faced, toward the dugout to get his glove. Casey Stengel stood on the dugout steps, his blue eyes blazing. He yelled at Mickey. Mantle was out of the game.

Mickey didn't try to excuse himself, or tell Casey that he'd thought there were two outs. He knew that every batter should go to the plate *knowing* how many outs there were. Mickey had no excuse.

He ducked into the dugout, trying to hide his face from fans and teammates. He remembered how hard Maris had slid into second to break up the double play. Rog had probably hurt his ribs sliding while Mickey loafed toward first. Mickey felt he had let Rog and the Yankees down.

The next day the newspapers printed black headlines: MANTLE BENCHED FOR NOT HUSTLING. That afternoon Mickey slunk into the clubhouse, worrying how his teammates would act toward him. The players immediately crowded around him. "Forget it, Mickey," said one. "I've forgotten how many outs there were a dozen times."

"So have I," said another player. Mickey knew they were fibbing. They were just trying to make him feel better. Well, he *did* feel better. And suddenly he knew how important he was to the other men on the club.

He had come to the Yankees a bashful nineteen-year-old, looking up in awe at DiMaggio and Rizzuto and all the famous players he had read about. Now, in 1960, Mantle was twenty-eight years old. And the younger Yankees — Tony Kubek, Bobby Richardson, and Clete Boyer — looked up to Mantle the way Mantle had once looked up to Di-Maggio.

Mickey realized suddenly that he could never let up, not just because of himself, but because of the way the other Yankees felt about him. They looked up to him as their leader. Even when he was in a slump, he helped his team by being in the line-up. And he wasn't having such a bad year after all, he realized. Weren't the Yankees in the thick of the race? He'd led them this far. He could go on being the leader even if he didn't hit a home run with men on base. He had to stop worrying about hitting home runs and simply play 100 per cent all the time.

Mickey was ready to start playing 100 per cent that next day. Would Casey let him play against the Orioles? First place was at stake. And besides, Mickey wanted to make up for yesterday's boner.

Casey put him in the line-up, but as Mickey ran out to center field, fans hooted, "Run it out, Mickey." People laughed. Mickey kept his head down.

His bat spoke for him. In the first inning

he rocketed a home run into the right-field bullpen.

The Orioles fought back to tie the score 1–1. That was the score as the Yankees came to bat in the last of the ninth. Up to the plate stepped Mickey, the big crowd up and yelling for him to come through, as he had come through so often in the past. The Oriole pitcher looked down, got the sign, reared back, and threw.

Mickey swung and the crowd knew, with that crack of bat, that Mickey Mantle had come through again. The ball soared into the seats. *Home run!* Mickey ran around the bases, wearing that Tom Sawyerish grin of his. And the Yankees won. They were back in first place.

Old Casey clapped his gnarled hands, while the Yankees rushed out to congratulate Mickey and escort him to the dugout. Yankee fans were roaring, roaring their praise loud and clear. Nobody — but nobody — was booing Mickey Mantle.

In the clubhouse Mickey said, "I wanted to have a good game more than I've ever wanted to have a good game in my life. When I came to the park I was hoping for something nice to happen. I never thought it would turn out as nice as it did."

In his biography, *Mickey Mantle: Mr. Yankee,* Al Silverman wrote: "It was Mickey's twenty-ninth home run of the year and it had marked a turning point for the Yankees and for Mickey Mantle. The Yankees were in first place again and Mickey was hot. From that August 15th to the end of the season, Mickey hit another eleven home runs. The Yankees beat off the challenge of the Orioles and then cooled off the White Sox. His forty home runs gave Mickey his third American League homer title. . . ."

The Yankees had won their eighth pennant in Mickey's ten years as a Yankee. But in the Series that year the Yankees faced the Pittsburgh Pirates. Before the Series opened, several of the Pirates made slurring remarks about the "so-so Yankees." Mickey burned to beat the Pirates. The Series went down to the seventh game — Mickey leading the way for the Yankees by pounding out 10 hits in 25 at-bats. He smacked 3 home runs, drove in 11 runs, and scored 8. But in the last of the ninth of the final game, the score tied, Bill Mazeroski hit a home run, and the Pirates ran off winners and world champions.

Mickey cried after that defeat. "I'm a sore loser," he said when he had regained his composure, "and I don't think that's bad. I don't think anyone should be happy to be a loser."

Casey Stengel's bosses also were not happy to lose. Shocking the baseball world, they fired Stengel, who had managed the team to ten pennants in twelve years. The new Yankee manager was a tough, cigar-smoking former Army major who had been a Yankee catcher, then a coach. His name was Ralph Houk, but the Yankees respectfully called him the Major.

At a press conference a reporter asked the Major how important Mickey was to the club.

"As Mantle goes," growled the Major, "so go the Yankees."

At the start of spring training for the 1961 season, Mickey came to camp very happy. He had just signed a contract for $75,000 — tops in baseball. Shortly after he arrived, he and Houk were talking. Houk told Mickey he wanted him to take charge of the Yankees.

"A team needs a leader," Houk explained later. "And Mantle has so much going for him. He's one ballplayer all the players like. They look up to him. I don't think he ever realized how much they do look up to him until last year."

Houk was right about Mickey. Ever since 1960, when he finally realized his importance to the team, Mantle had become more responsible and mature. The change in him showed in his reaction to Houk's suggestion about leading the Yankees. "This suddenly took me out of myself," Mickey recalled later, "and made me see that other people had problems and emotions. It just about put an end to my worst sulks and tantrums. I knew I was supposed to be setting the example."

At spring training in 1961, Mickey said to Clete Boyer, "I hope the Pirates win in the National League this year."

"Why?" asked Boyer.

"Because last year was the first time since I've been a Yankee that we lost a Series we should have won. I'd like to get even when we play in the Series this year."

Other Yankees, overhearing, nodded. They, too, hoped they'd meet the Pirates in the World Series.

But the season hadn't started. Would they be playing in the World Series? After all, to get into the Series, a team must first win the pennant. How could the Yankees be so sure they'd win that?

They were sure because Mickey Mantle, their leader, had said they'd play in the Series. And if Mickey said it was so, then it was so.

When the season started, Mickey's bat pointed the way to the Series. The Yankees won ten of their first sixteen games, and seven of those winning games were won on clutch hits by Mickey.

In Detroit the Yankees jumped into a 6–0 lead. The Tigers scratched back. As the Yankees came to bat in the top of the eighth, Detroit led 11–8.

Bobby Richardson singled and came around to score on a double by Tony Kubek. Up came Mickey, batting lefty. He slammed a long home run and the score was knotted 11–11.

In the tenth Mickey came to bat again, a runner on first. He leaned into a fast ball and ripped another home run and the Yankees went off 13–11 winners.

Early in May Mickey was leading the league in home runs with nine and he was hitting .325.

But as the Major had said, as Mickey goes, so go the Yankees — for better or worse. Mickey fell into a slump, his average diving to .279, and the Yankees lost five out of seven games.

Then the Tigers came roaring into Yankee Stadium, leading the league. In a doubleheader Mickey stroked five hits in eight at-bats, and the Yankees swept both games to bounce back into the pennant race.

By mid-July the Tigers and Yankees were locked in a furious pennant struggle. At the same time Mickey and his good friend, Yankee right fielder Roger Maris, were locked in another duel. Mickey and Roger shared the home run lead with thirty-five each. Both were seventeen games ahead of the pace set by Babe Ruth when the Bambino hit his historic sixty home runs.

Could Mick or Roger break the Babe's record?

Mickey hoped he could, but if he couldn't he hoped Roger could break it. But most important, he wanted to win that pennant and avenge last year's loss in the Series to the Pirates.

On September 1 the Tigers returned to Yankee Stadium, sniffing at the heels of the Yankees; they were only a game and a half from first place.

At that time Mickey, Roger Maris, and Bob Cerv were sharing an apartment on

Long Island. Their families had all returned home, since the children had to go to school. On the morning of the first of the three games with the Tigers, Cerv said to Mickey over breakfast, "How many games do you think we need?"

"If we can take just two of them," said Mickey, "they're going to have a rough time catching us."

Roger Maris nodded. "If we can take the first two games," he said, "I'll bet we will win the third."

The Yankees squeaked through to win the first game 1–0. In the second game, clawing to stay in the race, the Tigers leaped to a 2–0 lead. Then Mickey walked and Bill Skowron doubled him home. In the fourth Mickey dragged a bunt single, scoring Maris and tying the game 2–2.

In the sixth Mickey walked up to hit again. He swung downward on a pitch, and pain flashed through his left arm. Later, in the dugout, a trainer tested the arm and told Mickey he had pulled a muscle.

Houk kept Mickey in the game. "He was in pain," Houk told reporters later, "but I needed him in center field. He has become as important to this team on defense as he is on offense — that's how great an outfielder he

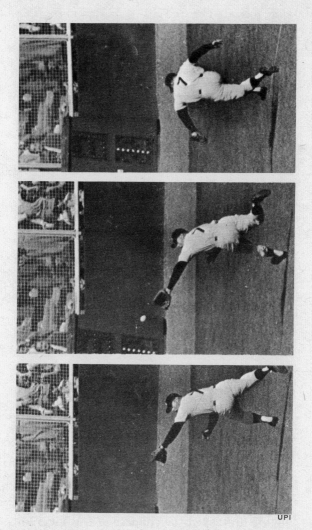

UPI

Of Mickey's once-poor fielding, Ralph Houk said, "He is as important on defense as on offense. That's how great a fielder he has become."

has become. With the score only 3–2, I couldn't chance taking him out of there."

The Yankees went on to win 7–2. Now it was the third and final game — the chance for the Yankees to win all three against the Tigers. "If you can play," the Major said to Mickey, "let me know."

Mickey said he could play. He borrowed one of Bob Cerv's heavy thirty-six ounce bats to slow down his swing as he didn't want to place more strain on the pulled muscle in his left arm. "I won't be able to swing a heavy bat as fast," he told Cerv. "I'll have to swing easier so I won't have as much pain when I miss."

In the first inning, swinging easy, Mickey drove a home run into the right-field stands and the Yankees led 2–0. The Tigers bounced back to take the lead 5–4, as the Yankees came to bat in the bottom of the ninth.

Mickey came to bat. Again with an easy swing of that heavy bat he drove another pitch into the seats to tie the game 5–5.

As Mantle goes, so go the Yankees.

The Yankees, inspired as they watched Mantle hit homers, even though he was in pain, rose up to beat the Tigers 8–5. That sweep destroyed the chances of the Tigers or of any other team to win the pennant. The

Yankees went on to win thirteen straight games and zoom far out in front in the race for the flag.

In the last month of that 1961 season, though, tension mounted as Roger and Mickey hit one home run after another in their pursuit of the Babe's record. At the time there was a popular movie called *Dial M for Murder* so as M & M (Maris and Mantle) cracked home runs, fans said of the pair: "Dial M for murder."

Some fans thought Mickey and Roger, chasing the same record, were jealous of each other. When people mentioned that to Bob Cerv, who was living with the two men, Bob laughed.

Mickey and Rog, said Bob in an article in *Sport* Magazine, constantly ribbed each other about the record. "If you hit your sixtieth," Roger told Mickey one day, "I'll ask the umpire to look at your bat and throw it out of the game if it's illegal."

"It would be foolish of me," wrote Cerv, "to say that Roger and Mickey weren't conscious of each other. They were. They both admitted many times that while they wished the other fellow luck, this was competition for the greatest honor in baseball. Mickey was rooting for Mickey and Roger was rooting for Roger. But that had nothing to do with the respect they had for one another.

"If there was any professional jealousy between them, they did a pretty good job of hiding it, I can tell you that."

On September 2 Mickey slammed his fifty-second homer of the season. With a month to go, he stood just eight home runs away from Ruth's record. As Mickey circled the bases after slamming that homer, some 40,-000 people in Yankee Stadium stood and yelled and clapped. "I've never heard so much cheering for me in all my years with the Yankees," Mickey said after the game. "They've never been so good to me."

There were no boos for Mickey now. Everyone was cheering for him to break Ruth's record. But while they cheered for Mickey, they booed Roger Maris. Roger was a new Yankee, a stranger, as Mickey had been new and a stranger in 1951. And what Joe DiMaggio had been to Yankee fans in 1951, Mickey Mantle was to Yankee fans in 1961. In 1951 they had cheered Joe and booed Mickey. In 1961 they booed Roger and cheered Mickey.

A very bad cold, though, sidelined Mickey in the home-run race. Then an infection opened a wound in his left thigh. By mid-

September he was on the bench. On September 25 he hit his fifty-fourth home run. That was his last home run of the 1961 season, in which he had hit .317 and driven in 128 runs. He went to the hospital, where surgeons operated on the infected thigh.

Maris, alone now, pursued the ghost of Ruth. There was the booing, the pressure, the constant strain of being asked, "Can you do it?" One day, before Mickey went to the hospital, Maris fled from the questioning and said to his good friend, "I can't take it any longer, Mick."

Mickey looked at him. "You'll have to take it, Rog," he said. "You'll just have to."

Roger nodded. And he stood up under the pressure, hitting his sixty-first home run in the Yankees' 162nd game. Ruth had hit sixty in 154 games, but Maris had hit more home runs than anyone in a baseball season.

And so the fierce M & M duel ended. Mantle said to Cerv, "Rog deserves all the credit in the world. I'm very happy for him."

In the National League the Cincinnati Reds had won the pennant. Mickey had lost his chance to beat the Pirates, but he could still get some satisfaction. If he beat the 1961 National League champions, the team

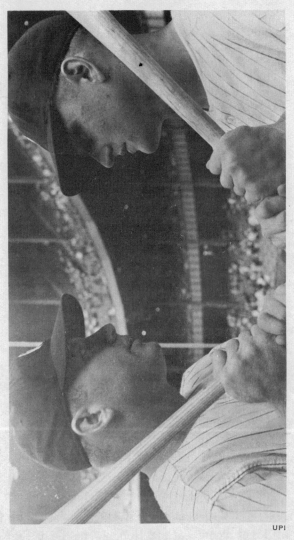

In 1961 Mickey (left) and Roger Maris fought a fierce but friendly contest to break the Babe Ruth home-run record.

that had finished ahead of the Pirates, he would have his revenge.

Since Mickey's thigh wound still had not healed, he sat in the dugout as the Yankees won the first game. The Reds won the second.

Mickey came out to play the third game and the Yankees won it. He didn't get a hit, but as Bobby Richardson once said, "We are a different ball club when he's in the line-up. It makes everyone feel we can win when Mickey is on our side."

In the fourth game Mickey drilled a sharp liner into left-center field. It was a sure double for someone with Mickey's speed, but he hobbled in pain to the first base. The wound had burst open.

Mickey had to leave the game. For him the Series was over, but that last hit had shown the Yankees the way.

The Yankees won that fourth game. And they won the fifth, winning the Series four games to one.

After that fifth game, Mickey rushed to the airport. A sportswriter saw him about to board a plane with his wife, Merlyn. Mickey smiled and said hello. And why shouldn't he have smiled — in spite of his pain? For the seventh time in his eleven years with the team, the Yankees were world champions.

10

Mick the Man:
Away from Baseball

MILLIONS OF FANS idolize Mickey Mantle. His teammates admire him and try to be like him. And in his own home, his four sons look up to their father just as the rookies do — and for the same reason. He is a good friend to them in every way he can be.

One October evening a few years ago, a friend drove with Mickey toward the Mantle home on the outskirts of Dallas, Texas. Mickey had moved from Commerce to Dallas to be close to the businesses he owned. There were oil wells, a bowling center, a motel; and he was part-owner of an insurance firm. Mickey, the one-time rookie who couldn't afford a new glove, was now making $100,000 a year in baseball and another $50,000 from his businesses.

As he drove toward home, Mickey explained that some of the businesses had been very successful, while some had failed. "All in all, though," said Mickey, "I'm going to be able to give my children the financial security I never had. They're never going to have to worry about money the way my dad had to worry and the way I had to worry."

Mickey turned into his driveway. As he turned off the engine, his two older sons, Mickey, Jr., and David, came running toward him.

"Let's play a game," hollered Mickey, Jr., waving a football.

"Okay," Mickey grinned.

The two boys and their father walked around to the grounds behind the house. There was almost enough grass for a football field.

Mickey, Jr., tossed the football to his father, then ran out for a pass with the speed of his grandfather, Mutt Mantle — the same speed Mickey Mantle had once had. Mickey flipped a long forty-yard pass to his son, who caught the ball over his shoulder.

"Just like Bob Hayes," yelled Mickey, Jr. Bob Hayes catches passes for the Dallas Cowboys, the Mantle family's home-town team.

Merlyn Mantle came out to watch. Slim and blonde, she still looked like the high

UPI

Mickey's biggest fans are his four sons, here in a 1964 picture: Danny, 4; Billy, 6; David, 8; and Mickey, Jr., 11.

school coed whom Mickey had met back in Oklahoma. Like many high school girls, Merlyn had known nothing about football or baseball. Though Mickey was a famous athlete at Commerce High School, Merlyn, who attended another high school a few miles away, had never heard of him. Mickey, though, had heard of *her*. Merlyn was as famous in her high school as Mickey was in his — for her baton-twirling. Merlyn also sang at church services and Mickey had heard about her fine voice.

Only after they were married did Merlyn learn the fine points of baseball and football. Later, during the baseball season, the Mantles would rent a house in New Jersey, only a short ride across the George Washington Bridge to Yankee Stadium. Merlyn and the boys would often go to see Mickey play, sitting in the special seats behind home plate reserved for the players' families. When the Yankees won and Mickey was hitting well, Merlyn and the boys would leave the ballpark smiling. But when the Yankees lost or Mickey's hitting was off, the ride home would be a silent one.

"When Mickey is in a slump or the Yankees lose," Merlyn once told a writer, "the children have learned to leave him alone. He sits glued to a chair, watching TV, a dark cloud around his head. His hay fever, always a nuisance, seems worse during a slump. Mostly, I leave him alone too."

But now they were back in Dallas. It was October, and baseball slumps were forgotten. Mickey threw spirals to his two older sons; and soon the younger boys, Billy and Danny, ran out to join the fun. For Mickey Mantle, this autumn evening, the only sport was football.

After a while, they went into the house for dinner. The boys washed up before they sat down at the table. They ate quietly while Mickey, at the head of the table, talked with them about what they had been doing all day.

After dinner Mickey and his sons flopped on the floor in front of a TV set. Every once in a while, Mickey would squeeze an arm of one of the boys, touch another on the foot, or pat one on the head. Like so many dads, he was showing his affection in a quiet way.

That night, after the children had gone to bed, some of Mickey's and Merlyn's friends came over for a small party. As in many homes, the men were on one side of the room talking sports, while the women gathered on the other side of the room and talked girl-talk.

Mickey was telling the men some of the funny things that can happen in a baseball season. Before the 1962 World Series between the Giants and the Yankees, he explained, reporters had been writing stories about how this Series would feature two of the greatest center fielders of all time: Willie Mays and Mickey Mantle.

"Well, you know what happened," Mickey was saying in his slow Oklahoma drawl. "Neither one of us was having a real good Series. So one day I'm in center field and I hear this big, booming voice yell at me, 'Hey, Mantle! Everyone came out here to see which was better, you or Mays. Now we wonder which is *worse!*'

"I just grinned and paid no attention to him," continued Mickey. "Then the next inning I grounded out and I was hitting .100 for the Series. I go back to the outfield and I hear this guy yell, 'Hey, Mantle, you win. *You're* the worst!'"

Mickey burst into laughter. This is the kind of baseball story Mickey likes best — the kind in which he comes out something less than a hero.

He told another story. "In a game I struck

out three times. When I got back to the clubhouse, I just sat down on a stool and held my head in my hands. I felt like crying.

"I heard someone come up next to me. It was little Timmy Berra, Yogi's son. He tapped me on the knee, softlike. I figured he was going to say something nice to me, you know, like 'You keep hanging in there,' or something like that.

"But little Timmy, he looks at me and he says, 'You *stink!*'" Again, Mickey shook with laughter.

Mickey told how Casey Stengel once put Billy Martin, who usually led off, in the seventh spot because Martin was in a slump. Martin, slump or not, thought he should have been batting fourth or fifth.

"Hey, Case," Martin yelled at Stengel, "how come you have me batting seventh? Pretty soon you'll have me batting behind the bat boy."

It was for Billy Martin that Mickey had named his son Billy. Martin was a Yankee second baseman. (Later he became a coach with the Minnesota Twins and, as of the end of 1968, the Twins' manager.) Tough and aggressive, Martin came to the Yankees as a rookie and snarled at veterans — men who had been in the big leagues for a dozen years.

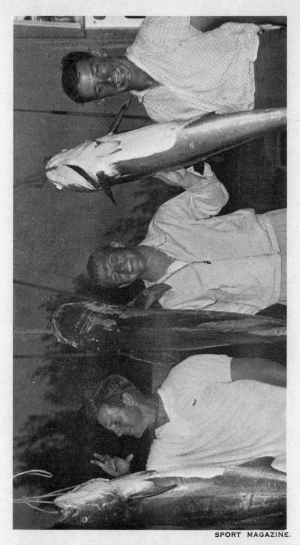

Whitey Ford (left), Mickey, and Billy Martin (right) formed
a lasting friendship while they were Yankee teammates.

The shy, bashful Mickey wouldn't even say hello to such men. Yet, as so often happens, these two opposites became good friends and often roomed together on the road.

Then Mickey told about another of his best friends, Whitey Ford. A blond, pug-nosed kid from the sidewalks of New York, Whitey pitched for the Yankees and soon became known as the best "money pitcher" in baseball.

A *money pitcher*. That's the kind you send out for the seventh game of a World Series — not just a twenty-game winner, though Whitey was that too — but the kind of pitcher who can go out under great pressure and win the *big* games. That was Whitey Ford.

Whitey was the laughing kind, needling people with pointed wisecracks, yelling friendly insults to teammates. Mickey was the kind who got laughs in a quiet way, with soft-spoken jokes and anecdotes. Yet these two, the city-boy Ford and the country-boy Mantle, were also good friends. And wherever the Yankees traveled, you would see the three of them together: Mantle, Ford, and Martin.

In 1957 the trio was broken up when Martin was traded but the three remained good friends.

Mickey's guests chuckled at his baseball stories. They relished his drawling way of telling them as much as the stories themselves.

After a while, Mickey stood up to go to the kitchen to get refreshments for his guests. There was an air of well-being about him. He looked relaxed and well-dressed.

Like most ballplayers, Mickey prefers casual clothes — slacks and sports jackets or cardigans — of good quality. As a miner's son, and as a young man working in the mines, he had worn patched clothes and cheap suits. Now he enjoyed being able to dress well and he found that being able to buy nice clothes for his wife and his sons was one of the greatest pleasures his money gave him.

Later, as his guests were getting ready to leave, someone asked Mickey if he hoped his sons would be big-league ballplayers.

"It would be nice," replied Mickey. "But you can't force it on them."

When he was reminded that the game had been forced on him by his father, Mickey said, "It would be different for my sons. People would get on them because of their name. That's what happened to my brothers."

His twin brothers, Roy and Ray, had played minor-league baseball.

"They're good athletes," Mickey said. "And they have the size — six-foot-one and 200 pounds. They just didn't really like the game a lot. If you don't like it, you got no business in it. Because even if you like it, it's tough to play."

This game, which Mickey liked so much, was soon going to be *very* tough — almost impossible — for Mickey himself to play.

11

Mickey Comes Back

IN 1962 MICKEY was named the American League's Most Valuable Player for the third time. He hit thirty home runs and batted .321 as the Yankees won their tenth pennant in his twelve years with the team. In the World Series the Yanks beat the Giants — now the San Francisco Giants — and Mickey had his eighth world championship ring.

Early in the 1963 season Mickey hit a ball harder than he — or perhaps anyone else — has ever hit a ball. Facing Kansas City's Bill Fischer, with the score tied 7–7 in the eleventh inning, Mickey came to bat left-handed. He leaned into a fast ball and drove it toward the right-field roof in Yankee Stadium.

"It's going out, it's going out," people yelled, staring at that soaring drive and remembering Mantle's almost over-the-roof hit in 1956.

This time the ball struck the facade eighteen inches below the roof — 374 feet from home plate, 106 feet above the ground.

A month later, though, in June, Mickey broke a bone in his leg trying to climb a wire fence to nab a long drive. For sixty-one games he was out of the line-up, while the bone mended. In August, still limping, he came to bat for the first time in two months. Some 40,000 people in Yankee Stadium stood and roared that day as Number 7 walked to plate; the fans were telling Mickey how glad they were to have him back.

Mickey had never heard such a thunderous tribute. He could feel the hair bristling on the back of his neck — he even had goose flesh. He *had* to hit the ball — a grounder, a pop-up, anything. He couldn't let these people down by striking out.

The Orioles led 10–9. Lefthander George Brunet whizzed a fast ball by Mickey for a strike. Mickey blinked. That pitch had seemed tremendously fast, for he hadn't seen a good fast ball in two months. Over and over Mickey kept repeating to himself: *Don't strike out!* He'd be so ashamed, disappointing all these people who were shouting their affection for him.

Brunet rifled his next pitch toward Mickey. Mickey swung and the ball shot on a rising line toward the left-field wall. People came to their feet, yelling. Back to the wall galloped the Oriole left fielder. Helplessly he watched the ball drop into the seats.

A Mantle home run! Mickey limped around the bases. People couldn't believe what they had seen. In *The Education of a Baseball Player*, Mickey called that home run the greatest thrill of all his baseball career. "I don't know," he wrote, "if I ran fast or slow or what. I'm glad I didn't fall down a couple of times. I told myself: 'I'm a lucky stiff. Gee, but I'm a lucky stiff.'"

A lucky stiff? Well, hardly. He had come back from an injury, just as he had come back from dozens of other painful injuries — this champion who should never have been.

He played in only 65 games in 1963, batting .314 and hitting 15 home runs. Again the Yankees won the pennant — their fourth in a row. In the Series, his knees encased, as they always were, in bandages, Mickey hit a home run off the Dodgers' fabled Sandy Koufax. But the Dodgers — now the Los An-

After a 61-game absence with a broken foot, Mickey limps to the plate and slams a home run in this game with Baltimore in 1963.

geles Dodgers — overwhelmed the Yankees by winning four games in a row. "This was the worst beating I had ever seen the Yankees take," Mickey wrote in *The Education of a Baseball Player*, "and it left me aching for another crack at this club."

But that was not to happen.

The next season, 1964, Mickey hit .303 with 35 home runs as the Yankees swept to their fifth straight pennant — and Mickey's twelfth in his fourteen years with the Yankees. By now he held a long string of World Series records:

Most runs scored . . . most runs batted in . . . most total bases . . . most long hits . . . most extra bases on long hits . . . most bases on balls . . . most strikeouts . . . most Series games played in by an outfielder.

During the 1964 Series against the Cardinals, Mickey set another record. In the fifth game, with the score tied 1–1 in the last of the ninth, Mickey slammed a long home run off Barney Schultz to win the game 2–1 for the Yankees. This was Mickey's sixteenth World Series homer, breaking a record set by the great Babe Ruth. He hit two more homers, but the Cardinals won the Series.

In 1965 Johnny Keane came over from the Cardinals to manage the Yankees. Mickey, with his shoulder and knees aching, struggled through a tough season for himself and the team. He hit only .255 and 19 home runs. The once-powerful Yankee team had fallen down badly and finished in sixth place. But Mickey Mantle had become a legend.

He was a legend with the Yankees in the way a brave captain can be a legend to his troops. If the captain charges into heavy fire, his troops follow. His bravery is transmitted to them, and they become brave men. Somehow Mickey's skills were transmitted to the rest of the Yankees, and his skills made them more skillful players.

"During games," said Tony Kubek, the Yankees' former shortstop, "Mickey would yell at me from the top step of the dugout, rooting for me to get a base hit. You always heard Mantle above all the other voices. I don't know why. But he made you bear down. He made you concentrate, and when you're concentrating, you got a much better chance of getting a hit."

Mantle's opponents, too, regarded his skills with awe. Shortstop Dick Howser, then with Cleveland, said, "So far I've been on two big-league ball clubs, but I've yet to be on a ball club that caught Mickey Mantle stealing a base!"

Of Mickey's hitting, pitcher Jim (Mudcat) Grant told this story about Mantle when Grant was with the Indians. "We're ahead 1–0 in the bottom of the fourth when a gale starts blowing in from the outfield — lots of wind and rain. The Yankees get a man on base. The umpires don't hold up the game because there are two out.

"Well, Mickey comes up and count goes to three balls and two strikes. Now the gale is really roaring in, wind and rain smacking Mickey right in the face. I can see he's having trouble seeing with all that water being splattered in his eyes. I figure I'll throw my best pitch — my fast ball — and Mickey isn't going to see it in the rain. I throw the ball just where I want it — low and outside. I don't know how he ever touched it. But Mickey knocks that ball 400 feet into the teeth of that gale, right into the bullpen for a home run. The next inning they call the game and we lose 2–1."

Ballplayers — strong men themselves — never stop being amazed at Mickey's great strength, in the field as well as at-bat. "Nobody ever hit me harder than when Mantle knocked me down in a World Series," said

PeeWee Reese, the old Dodger shortstop, looking back on twenty years of being flipped at second base. "I got up and started for the dugout, my bones stinging, and I thought, 'You'll never make it to the dugout, you'll never make it.'"

Yes, Mickey had won the respect and admiration of the ballplayers, and he had become the idol of the New York fans. For years, the Yankee front office pleaded with Mickey: "We want to have a Mickey Mantle Day for you at Yankee Stadium. Let us do it."

Mickey had said no. He didn't want people giving him gifts. It wasn't right, not with his making so much money. He didn't want to do that. But the fans wanted to give Mantle a day and finally in 1965 Mickey agreed.

On a broiling hot late-summer day in 1965 some 50,000 fans came to Yankee Stadium to pay tribute to their favorite ballplayer. It was Mickey Mantle Day.

Mickey stepped out onto the field. The Yankee players lined up along one foul line. The Tiger players lined up along another foul line. By tradition, this is the ballplayers' salute to the greatness of one of their own.

At home plate Mickey's fans had stacked

On Mickey Mantle Day, Mickey and Joe DiMaggio greet the fans. As a rookie, Mickey was awed by the great DiMag.

hundreds of gifts. At Mickey's insistence, these gifts were later shipped to charities. Mickey accepted the gifts, the crowd roaring in wave after wave, saying with cheers what they could not say in words: *We love you, Mickey*.

Now Mickey stepped up to the microphone, the huge crowd suddenly hushing, waiting to hear what he would say.

"I wish I had another fifteen years to play," Mickey said, that husky drawl booming through the silent Stadium. "When I walk down the street and people stop me and say, 'Hi, Mick,' and 'How's your leg?' and things like that, it makes it all worthwhile."

Then Mickey said thanks. The fans roared their affection. Mickey turned and grinned, embarrassed as a new boy in school. He rubbed at something glimering around his eyes. The crowd roared on — for minutes, by actual count — and their roaring told Mickey that the fans, too, wished he could play another fifteen years.

But he couldn't. He knew it, they knew it. The big question was: Could he play more than another year or two?

12

New Challenge for Mickey

ICKEY WENT HOME to Dallas, planning to exercise his shoulder and knees. He hoped to be in top shape for 1966. One day he went out into the yard to play touch football with his sons. Playing all-out, as he did in everything, Mickey lunged as one of the boys dodged away. Suddenly pain shot through his right shoulder.

That night Mickey told a friend: "I'm through as a ballplayer. I could hardly throw a ball last year, my right shoulder ached so badly. I know I wrecked the shoulder out there today. Next year I won't be able to throw at all."

Mickey phoned Ralph Houk, who was now the Yankee general manager, to say that he was going to retire from baseball. Houk pleaded with Mickey: "Come to New York and talk it over." At last, Mickey agreed.

When Mickey came to New York he was sure he would never play again. But Houk persuaded him to fly to the famous Mayo Clinic. There specialists examined the aching shoulder. After days of tests, the specialists astonished Mickey. Yes, they said, he could go on playing baseball — after surgery. So they operated on the shoulder and repaired the damage.

In 1966 Mickey came back to play baseball, and Ralph Houk came out of the front office to take over again as the team's manager, replacing Keane.

Houk talked bravely about rebuilding a team whose greatest players had grown old or retired. The key man of the new team, Houk said, would be Mickey Mantle. Even a Mantle with bad knees, said Houk, could lift the Yankees.

"Mickey's a real holler guy on the bench," said Houk. "He does things to everyone on the team. The other players sit there and hear Mantle pulling for a base hit. They just have to give their best."

Mickey hit .288 and 23 home runs. Only four American League players hit more home runs, only four batted higher. And he played 108 games in the outfield without committing a single error.

Mickey signs his 1966 contract for "The Major," Ralph Houk,
after undergoing surgery to repair a severe shoulder injury.

But Mickey often had to be lifted from games in the late innings. Three operations had cut out most of the cartilage in his knees. Cartilage is the "cushion" of the knees. Without that cushion, as one Yankee said, "you're rubbing bone on bone when you run."

"I used to love to run," Mickey said in 1966. "It was fun to run. Now it hurts. The knees hurt after a game. They'll hurt when I go to bed tonight. Sometimes I'm lucky if the pain is gone when I wake up in the morning."

Despite the pain, Mickey ran. When he got on base, overconfident first basemen would play deep, figuring they didn't have to keep Mickey close. After all, he had bad wheels, as ballplayers call their legs. Then Mickey would take off and steal second, grimacing with pain.

As Johnny Keane had said: "Of course I don't want to send him down to second on those legs. But telling him not to run is like talking to that wall over there."

But by the end of the 1966 season, the once-fantastic speed of Mantle had been cut in half. Knees riddled by injuries, Mickey couldn't cover center field nor could he dash in from left or right for bails hit in front of him.

If he couldn't play the outfield, where could he play? Once he had been a short-stop, but Casey Stengel said his hands were too slow to snatch at balls that took a bad hop. He had played third base in one game as a Yankee and bobbled two of four ground balls.

Where could he play? Ralph Houk had an idea: he would try Mickey at first base.

One reporter wrote: "Mickey will get killed playing first base. Someone will collide with him and wreck his career right there. And how about all those sudden starts and stops a first baseman must make? They'll be murder on his knees."

Mickey, too, doubted he could play first base. His idol, Joe DiMaggio, had once tried to play first base late in his career. He played one game, then threw away the first baseman's mitt, and ran back to center field. Joe wanted no part of first base.

If DiMag couldn't play first, how could Mickey? "But if Ralph wants me to," said Mickey, "I'll try it for a few weeks at the start of spring training. But I'll tell you the truth: I've never played there before. I don't even have a first baseman's glove."

"That's O.K.," said Houk, grinning. "If you learn how to play first, I'll buy the glove."

At spring training at Fort Lauderdale, Florida, before the 1967 season, Mickey told writers he hoped he could play somewhere for the Yankees. He had some goals he wanted to reach. He wanted to play in more games than any other Yankee, breaking Lou (The Iron Man) Gehrig's record of 2,164. Mickey had played in 2,113 — 51 short of that record. Then he wanted to hit 500 home runs — he had 496.

Would he reach those goals? Many doubted that he could go on playing.

13

Who Is Half as Good as Mickey?

IN THE FIRST DAY of the 1967 spring training at the Yankee camp in Fort Lauderdale, two New York reporters expressed their doubts about Mickey's future. They were watching Mickey warm up on the sideline, catching throws with a first baseman's mitt. "I predict that if Mickey tries to play first base he will be seriously hurt before he has played five games," said one of the writers.

"I agree," said the other. "It's a 1,000-to-1 shot that a thirty-five-year-old guy, with bad knees, can learn a new position. Mickey will see first base this year — but only as a base runner."

"If he can't play first base, where can he play?" asked the first newsman. "You may be seeing the last days of Mickey Mantle."

Mickey himself shared their doubts, even though a few weeks earlier he had signed a

$100,000 Yankee contract for the fifth successive year. When the writers asked him about playing first base, he said, with his Tom Sawyer grin, "I just hope that in the ninth inning of a close game nobody hits a ground ball at me."

"I don't know what will happen and neither does Mickey," said Ralph Houk. "It will be interesting to see. If it doesn't work out, then Mickey goes right back to center field and Joe Pepitone moves back to first base."

The Major paused, drawing on a huge cigar. "I am convinced," he said, "that having less running to do will make Mickey's legs stronger and keep him in the line-up more regularly. Every time we have his bat in the line-up we have a better chance of winning."

Now, on this hot day at Fort Lauderdale, Mickey was going to try fielding ground balls at first base for the first time in his career. After warming up on the sideline, Mickey suddenly waved to coach Frank Crosetti. "Hit me some!" yelled Mickey, and he ran to first base.

Photographers circled Mickey, cameras poised. Crosetti hit a skipping grounder. Mickey fielded the ball cleanly, despite the popping of flashbulbs in his eyes.

For ten minutes he scooped up grounders. Later he said, "It felt much more natural than I expected. I think I'm going to be all right. This could add two or three years to my career. The stopping and starting, I think, is no tougher than in the outfield, and there is a lot less running."

Someone suggested he would be smart not to strain his knees by lunging at balls hit too far away from him. Mickey looked at the man in amazement. "If I get a chance at a ball," he said, "I'm going to try to catch it — no matter what."

Mickey set a deadline for himself. If he could not play first base acceptably by the end of spring training, he would try to play center field or retire. "I want to be good at it," he told some friends. "I would never want to be embarrassed by playing it so bad the fans would get on me."

By the end of March, Mickey was snatching up ground balls with the expertness of Joe Pepitone. "I can't rush in on those bunts the way Joe does," Mickey said one day in the clubhouse, grinning. "But I think I'm doing all right."

He looked across the clubhouse where Pepitone was carefully combing his hair.

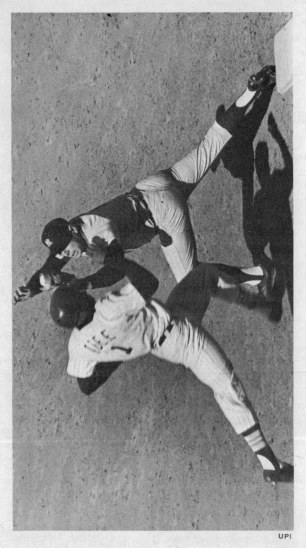

Playing first base to save his knees, Mickey continues to lunge forward in plays like this one, in spite of the pain.

"And I'm better looking," he added, laughing now.

With Mickey opening at first base and Pepitone in center field, the Yankees started the 1967 season with a rush, running close to the leaders. But Mickey, concentrating so hard on his fielding at first, couldn't buy a base hit, as the ballplayers say. After twelve games Mickey had knocked in only one run. His batting average was a pitiful .215.

The California Angels came to New York. In the third inning, the score tied 1–1 and a runner on first base, Mickey walked to the plate. Some 12,000 fans in Yankee Stadium unleashed an affectionate roar as Mickey stepped into the batter's box. On the mound the veteran Jack Sanford looked down for the sign. He went into his windup, threw a fast ball. Mickey swung, belting the ball on a line over second base. The center fielder took off for the bleacher wall. Then turned to watch the ball clear the thirteen-foot wall and smack into a bleacher seat — 415 feet from home plate.

Mickey trotted around the bases, the crowd shrieking excitement as though this had been a game-winning home run in the World Series. As Mickey said later, "People are happy to see me hit a home run because they're always afraid it might be my last."

It wasn't his last; it was far from his last. It was his first of the 1967 season and the 497th of his seventeen-year career.

In the fifth inning, Mickey came to bat again — two men on base, two out. He stroked a single into right field, scoring another run. The Yankees were on their way to a 5–2 victory. "It's good to see the big guy get going," Houk said after the game. "He's fielding at first base better than we ever expected. Now that he's hitting, he could pick up the club. He's still the leader."

"Yeah," Mickey was saying at the other end of the clubhouse, "I was getting worried about my hitting. When you're thirty-five and you go oh-for-twenty at-bats, you start thinking, 'Uh-uh, this might be it.'

"After those hits today, though, I feel better. Now I'll go up there and I'll think: I'm going to get a hit. That's half the game — thinking you are going to get a hit."

A few days later Mickey hit home run number 499. For the next week, whenever he came to bat, fans screamed for him to hit number 500. Mickey felt the pressure mounting, weighing him down. Naturally he wanted to please the fans, knowing they had come to see that 500th home run. But ballplayers will tell you: if you swing for a home run, you're not likely to hit one. And for more than a week, Mickey didn't.

Then Sunday, May 14, the Baltimore Orioles were the opponents at Yankee Stadium. Late in the game, with the Yankees leading 5–4 Mickey came to bat against Stu Miller. The crowd could not expect that home run from Mickey now. In some four years of trying, Mickey had never hit a home run off Miller who threw dancing pitches, once described as "slow, slower, and even slower."

The count went to three and two. Miller threw up a lazy curve ball. Batting left-handed, Mickey stepped into the pitch, lashing at the ball with all the power in those bull-like shoulders. *Whack!* The ball screamed toward the right-field seats, arching far over the Oriole right fielder's glove, and dropping into the hands of an overjoyed fan.

Mickey trotted around the bases. This was his 500th, but he ran out the homer as he ran out all his homers — head down, lips tight to hold in the joy he felt. At third base the coach, Frank Crosetti, reached out and shook Mickey's hand — something Cro rarely did.

Mickey ran to the dugout with the fans

still roaring knowing that now he was the sixth player in baseball history who had hit 500 home runs. The other five were: Babe Ruth (714), Willie Mays (542 at the end of 1966), Jimmy Foxx (534), Ted Williams (521), and Mel Ott (511).

"He didn't say a word," his pal, Whitey Ford, said later. "He was just pale as a ghost."

The next Yankee batter stepped up to hit. But the crowd kept roaring, a tumult so loud that Stu Miller couldn't pitch. He stood off the mound, waiting, and for minutes the crowd let Mickey know how much they thought of his feat. They kept on yelling while Mickey paced the dugout, too excited to sit down.

Finally the cheering died away. The game went on, the Yankees now leading 6–4. In the eighth the Orioles put men on first and second. Brooks Robinson tapped a ball to the shortstop, who stepped on second and threw to Mickey at first for the double play that would end the inning.

Mickey dropped the ball! Then still shaken by that home run, he threw wild to home, and a runner scored.

Now the score was 6–5, and the tying run was on second base. Suddenly it seemed that

Mickey Mantle, Hero, would become Mickey Mantle, Goat. But the Yankee pitcher snuffed out the next four Oriole batters and the Yankees were winners.

In the clubhouse Mickey shook his head. "If I'd lost the game on that error," he said, "I'd be hard to talk to. I'd be hiding somewhere — home run or no home run."

How did he feel after hitting the homer? "It felt," answered Mickey, "like when you win a World Series — a big load off your back. I wasn't really tense about hitting it, but about everybody *writing* about it. The team wasn't doing well and everywhere you'd see: 'When Is Mantle Going to Hit 500?' They talked about the home run instead of about the Yankees winning or losing. Now maybe we can get back to wining."

By June of 1967 Mickey, to save his strength, was sitting out the second games of most double-headers. On June 14, after playing in the first game, he came up to bat to pinch hit in the second. As he walked to the plate at D. C. Stadium in Washington, the announcer's voice crackled, "Ladies and gentlemen, batting for New York, Number 7, Mickey Mantle."

The Washington fans cheered loudly, for

in every city in the American League Mickey was as admired as he was in New York. On a three-and-two pitch, Mickey flied out.

As Mickey trotted toward the dugout, the announcer's voice boomed through the stadium, "With that at-bat, ladies and gentlemen, Mickey Mantle has played in 2,165 games as a New York Yankee — a new Yankee record, breaking the one set by Lou Gehrig."

The Washington fans came to their feet, applauding the greatness of Mickey Charles Mantle. Despite two bad knees and dozens of injuries, Mickey had broken the record of the Iron Man.

Later Mickey said, "Sure, it's a thrill when these things happen. Anytime you are the first to do something, you have to feel good. You don't think too much about it while you are playing, but I know I'll get a kick and a lot of great memories out of it later."

He paused, staring at his scuffed baseball shoes. "It took me more years than it took Lou, I know. But I don't think that takes any of the shine off my record. Of course, it might be that this is my last game and I only beat him by one. But I hope I will add enough games to the record to make it almost impossible for anyone to top me in the future."

Mickey had played more games as a Yankee than anyone — Gehrig, Ruth, DiMaggio, Berra. And he had hit his 500th home run. He had reached the two goals he had set for himself.

But there were other goals to reach, other ghosts to pass. Baseball is a game that never lets its great ones rest. Always there are new records to break, new marks to set.

On July 4 the Yankees, mired deep in eighth place, came to Minnesota to play a double-header against the Twins. In the first game, batting left-handed against Mudcat Grant, Mickey sliced a 370-foot home run to left center. It was his fifteenth of the season, the 511th of his career — tying Mel Ott.

In the eighth Mickey came to bat again and hit a 350-foot drive over the right-field screen — number 512. Mickey now stood fifth on the list of home-run kings.

Mickey circled the bases as the Twins' fans cheered. Mickey tipped his cap; his face was grim. He was happy about the home run, but the two homers had been the entire Yankee attack. The Twins won 8–3.

No, the ninth-place Yankees were certainly not the great team they once had been. Their younger players failed to do what Houk hoped they would. Their veterans — Tom Tresh, Joe Pepitone — limped with injuries. Mickey's legs ached. Yet he was to the Yankees what he had always been — their leader. Of the thirty-six games won by the Yankees in the first half of the 1967 season, Mickey drove home the winning run in eleven of them.

Someone looked up the figures for the first half of the season. Mickey led the team in home runs. He led in runs-batted-in. He led in runs scored. He led in bases on balls. And he had played in 75 of 81 games.

"Mantle has been the Yanks' MVP," wrote newspaperman Jim Ogle. "But what's new about that?"

In the second half of the season the Yankees stayed deep in the second division, finishing a bad ninth.

"I would hate to think I won't hit nine home runs the whole second half of the season," Mickey told Jim Ogle. Mickey was silent a few moments, then he talked about what might stop him from hitting those nine home runs.

"My legs have been aching," he told Ogle. "At times it feels as if I'm dragging two bowling balls with me when I go out to play first base. I know I couldn't play the outfield the way my legs feel. But I can get by at first base."

Those aching legs limited Mickey to 69 games in the second half of the 1967 season, and in many of those games he appeared only as a pinch hitter. He hit only six home runs in the last half of the season — three fewer than he needed to tie Williams. He finished with 22 home runs and hit only .245.

Yet, for someone who had thought two years earlier that he was finished in baseball, it had been a fine year. Mickey had appeared in 144 games and no one on the team played in more. He had played in more games, in fact, than in any other season since 1961.

Then the season was over. As Mickey dressed in the Yankee clubhouse, he felt very good. He had faced a challenge, playing first base, and conquered the challenge. "First base still has some problems," he was saying, "like bunts and pop fouls. I have trouble getting to them with these knees of mine. But last spring training I had doubts about playing first base. Now I've done it."

Mickey knotted his tie, ready now to leave the Yankee clubhouse and go home to his

UPI

Mickey puts the tag on Detroit's Al Kaline. Once Kaline
told a fan, "Nobody is half as good as Mickey Mantle."

family in Dallas. "See you next year," he said to several of the Yankees — and for the first time in many seasons, Mickey could be certain he would return. He wasn't through yet.

Late in the 1967 season, Al Kaline, the star right fielder for the Detroit Tigers, talked to a group of young fans. One boy, not as polite as he might have been, said to Kaline after the talk, "You're not half as good as Mickey Mantle."

Kaline smiled.

"Nobody," said Al Kaline, "is half as good as Mickey Mantle."

14

The Records of Mickey Mantle

IT WAS MAY 30, 1968, and at Yankee Stadium there was a Memorial Day doubleheader between the Yankees and the Senators. Some 28,000 fans cheered as Mickey walked up to the plate in the first inning of the opening game.

There was a runner on first base. On the mound for the Senators was Joe Coleman. Young Coleman had struck out Mickey four times in a game a week earlier. Coleman threw fast balls as swift as lightning bolts, and Mickey, at thirty-six, was not getting his bat off his shoulder quickly enough to meet them.

Coleman threw a fast ball. Mickey swung, this time lashing at the pitch with his old-time quickness. The ball shot on a rising line into the right-field stands. Home run! The Yankees led 2–0.

In the third, Mickey singled. When Joe Pepitone followed with a double, Mickey dashed all the way from first to score, running like the Mickey Mantle of ten years earlier. Now the Yankees led 3–0

In the fifth, Mickey hit another home run, the 524th of his career, and the Yankees led 4–0

In the sixth, with the Yankees now ahead 6–1, Mickey came up to bat for the fourth time. He lined his fourth hit, a double, down the right-field line, driving in another run.

In the eighth inning, Mickey came up to hit for the fifth time. The crowd stood and cheered as his name was announced. Mickey had gone four-for-four, and this crowd, with its cheering, was pleading for Mickey to get a fifth hit for a perfect day.

There were runners on first and second, one out. Big Jim Hannan was now on the mound for the Senators. He threw a dipping slider. Mickey snapped his bat at the pitch, driving the ball over the shortstop's head.

A single! It had driven in his fifth run. And Mickey had gone five-for-five!

Mickey stood on first base, hands on hips. The crowd's roaring poured down on him. In the Yankee dugout there was a flurry of action. Then a pinch runner dashed up the steps and ran out to take Mickey's place on the bag. Mickey trotted toward the dugout, the acclaim as loud as for any home run he had ever hit.

Never in Mickey's eighteen-year career had he accomplished more at the plate. In this 13–4 Yankee triumph, Mickey had socked five hits in five at-bats, rare for anyone and only the third time for Mickey in the big leagues. And never before had he driven in five runs.

Early in the 1968 season newspaperman Jim Ogle asked Mickey to list the five biggest thrills of his big-league career. Mickey picked these five, though not in any order:

1. His pinch-hit home run against Baltimore in 1963.

2. Mickey Mantle Day.

3. "The first time I stepped onto the field in Yankee Stadium in a Yankee uniform."

4. His ninth-inning home run off Barney Schultz that won the game against the Cardinals in the 1964 Series.

5. "Every time the fans give me a standing ovation."

There were many such ovations in every city of the American League during that season — not for any one thing Mickey did, but for all the things he had done in his brilliant career. And there was still another triumph waiting for Mickey in 1968.

Earlier in the season, Mickey had hit the four home runs he needed to pass Ted Williams' record; but as the season moved toward its close, he still needed one more home run to triumph over Jimmy Foxx's record of 534.

On September 19 the Yankees were in Detroit. The score stood 6–1 in favor of the Tigers with just two innings left to play. Denny McLain, pitching for Detroit, felt he had the game in the bag. It would be his thirty-first win of the season — a win that would break a thirty-seven-year-old record set by Lefty Grove. And as for the American League pennant . . . the Tigers had already wrapped it up. Out on the mound, McLain was happy and relaxed.

Now Mickey stepped into the batter's box. The crowd knew that he was just one home run short of the record-breaking 535th. Denny McLain knew it too.

Then an extraordinary thing happened. No one will ever be able to prove it, but here's how the legend will read:

McLain had pitched two strikes to Mickey

September 19, 1968, Mickey belts his record-breaking 535th home run off a pitch by Detroit's Denny McLain (number 17).

— fast balls over the inside corner. Then Mickey looked up at McLain and seemed to give him a signal. Instead of firing another hard one, McLain seemed almost to *toss* his next pitch over the plate — a medium fast ball, knee high. Mickey swung and connected, and the ball blasted out over right field and into the stands.

"Thanks!" yelled Mantle to McLain, and he toured the bases as 9,000 Detroit fans cheered.

"McLain has made a fan of me for life," Mickey grinned after the game.

But when reporters asked Denny if he had *given* the hit to Mickey, he denied it.

"I didn't throw it to him," Denny said. "It was a good pitch, a fast ball low. . . . But that Mantle — he was my idol!"

Now Mickey stood third on the list of all-time home-run kings — just behind Babe Ruth, with 714 homers, and Willie Mays, who had 585 on the day Mickey slugged his 535th.

Mickey and Willie had broken into baseball in that same far-off 1951 season. But Willie had come to bat far more often than Mickey, who had been out with injuries so many seasons. Willie, in fact, had close to a thousand more at-bats than Mickey from 1951 to 1968.

Mickey hit a home run, on the average, every fourteen times he came to bat. Willie hit a home run every fifteen times at bat. If Mickey had batted those thousand extra times that Willie had batted, it can be assumed, mathematically, he would have hit around seventy more home runs, putting him twenty to thirty home runs ahead of Willie.

But Willie *did* bat those thousand more times. So Willie Mays will be second on the all-time list of home-run hitters, and Mickey will stand behind him. As Mickey himself would tell you, *if's* don't count.

The fans know that one day soon Mickey will announce his retirement from baseball.

"Sometimes I think they feel sorry for me," said Mickey, "sorry that I've been hurt, sorry that I won't be playing for too much longer. But I don't want sympathy."

Mickey was silent a moment. "They talk about how great I might have been if I hadn't been hurt," he went on. "Gee, considering everything, I don't think I've had too bad a career."

Indeed it hasn't been too bad a career.

UPI

Met manager Gil Hodges presents a portrait to Mickey. The 1968 painting by Vic Mikuch shows Mickey with Billy, 10; his wife Merlyn; Mickey, Jr., 15; Danny, 8; and David, 12.

When he retires Mickey will hold more records than most people could count.

Not only does Mickey rank third on the list of home-run greats, but his bat has been so dreaded by pitchers that only two other hitters, Babe Ruth and Ted Williams, have received more walks.

Mickey's World Series records alone make a page in the history of baseball: most home runs (18) . . . most runs scored (42) . . . most runs batted in (40) . . . most total bases (123) . . . most bases on balls (43).

In 1956 he won the Triple Crown — for home runs, batting average, and runs-batted-in.

In three seasons (1956, 1957, and 1962) Mickey was voted the American League's Most Valuable Player — the third man in history to win the honor three times.

In four seasons (1955, 1956, 1958, and 1960) he was the American League's home run champion.

Not too bad a career?

It has been a superb career — especially for a champion who never should have been.

MICKEY MANTLE'S RECORD

Born on October 20, 1931, in Spavinaw, Oklahoma. Resides in Dallas, Texas.
Height, 6:00. Weight, 194 pounds. Gray eyes and blond hair. Bats left and right.
Throws right. Married; father of four boys: Mickey, Jr., David, Billy, and Danny.

Year	Club	Pos.	G	AB	R	H	2B	3B	HR	RBI	BB	SO	BA
1949	Independ.	SS	89	323	54	101	15	7	7	63	52	66	.313
1950	Joplin	SS	137	519	*141	*199	30	12	26	136	94	90	*.383
1951	New York	OF	96	341	61	91	11	5	13	65	43	74	.267
	Kansas City	OF	40	166	32	60	9	3	11	50	23	30	.361
1952	New York	OF-3B	142	549	94	171	37	7	23	87	75	•111	.311
1953	New York	OF-SS	127	461	105	136	24	3	21	92	79	90	.295
1954	New York	OF-IF	146	543	*129	163	17	12	27	102	102	*107	.300
1955	New York	OF-SS	147	517	121	158	25	•11	*37	99	*113	97	.306
1956	New York	OF	150	533	*132	188	22	5	*52	*130	112	99	*.353
1957	New York	OF	144	474	*121	173	28	6	34	94	*146	75	.365
1958	New York	OF	150	519	*127	158	21	1	*42	97	*129	•120	.304
1959	New York	OF	144	541	104	154	23	4	31	75	94	*126	.285
1960	New York	OF	153	527	*119	145	17	6	*40	94	111	*125	.275
1961	New York	OF	153	514	•132	163	16	6	54	128	*126	112	.317
1962	New York	OF	123	377	96	121	15	1	30	89	*122	78	.321
1963	New York	OF	65	172	40	54	8	0	15	35	40	32	.314
1964	New York	OF	143	465	92	141	25	2	35	111	99	102	.303
1965	New York	OF	122	361	44	92	12	1	19	46	73	76	.255
1966	New York	OF	108	333	40	96	12	1	23	56	57	76	.288
1967	New York	1B	144	440	63	108	17	0	22	55	107	113	.245
1968	New York	1B	144	435	57	103	14	1	18	54	106	97	.237
M. L. Totals			2401	8102	1677	2415	344	72	536	1509	1734	1710	.298

World Series Record

Year	Club	Pos.	G	AB	R	H	2B	3B	HR	RBI	BB	SO	BA
1951	New York	OF	2	5	1	1	0	0	0	0	2	1	.200
1952	New York	OF	7	29	5	10	1	1	2	3	3	4	.345
1953	New York	OF	6	24	3	5	0	0	2	7	3	8	.208
1955	New York	OF-PH	3	10	1	2	0	0	1	1	0	2	.200
1956	New York	OF	7	24	6	6	1	0	3	4	6	5	.250
1957	New York	OF-PH	6	19	3	5	0	0	1	2	3	1	.263
1958	New York	OF	7	24	4	6	0	1	2	3	7	4	.250
1960	New York	OF	7	25	8	10	1	0	3	11	8	9	.400
1961	New York	OF	2	6	0	1	0	0	0	0	0	2	.167
1962	New York	OF	7	25	2	3	1	0	0	0	4	5	.120
1963	New York	OF	4	15	1	2	0	0	1	1	1	5	.133
1964	New York	OF	7	24	8	8	2	0	3	8	6	8	.333
W. S. Totals			65	230	42	59	6	2	18	40	43	54	.257

* — Denotes led league.
• — Tied for league lead.

All-Star Game Record

Year	Club	Pos.	G	AB	R	H	2B	3B	HR	RBI	BB	SO	BA
1952	American	—		(selected, but did not play)									
1953	American	OF		2	0	0	0	0	0	0	1	0	.000
1954	American	OF		5	1	2	0	0	0	0	0	1	.400
1955	American	OF		6	1	2	0	0	1	3	0	1	.333
1956	American	OF		4	1	1	0	0	1	1	0	3	.250
1957	American	OF		4	1	1	0	0	0	0	1	1	.250
1958	American	OF		2	0	1	0	0	0	0	2	0	.500
1959	American	OF	2	3	0	1	0	0	0	0	1	1	.333
1960	American	OF	2	4	0	1	0	0	0	0	2	1	.250
1961	American	OF	2	6	0	0	0	0	0	0	1	3	.000
1962	American	OF	1	1	0	0	0	0	0	0	1	1	.000
1963	American	—		(selected, but did not play)									
1964	American	OF	1	4	1	1	0	0	0	0	0	2	.250
1965	American	—		(selected, but did not play)									
1967	American	PH		1	0	0	0	0	0	0	0	1	.000
1968	American	PH	1	1	0	0	0	0	0	0	0	1	.000
A. S. Totals			16	43	5	10	0	0	2	4	9	16	.233